CAVALIER KING CHARLES SPANIEL

LAURA LANG

Cavalier King Charles Spaniel

Editor: Stephanie Fornino
Indexer: Elizabeth Walker
Series Designer: Mary Ann Kahn
Book Designer: Angela Stanford

TFH Publications®
President/CEO: Glen S. Axelrod
Executive Vice President: Mark E. Johnson
Publisher: Christopher T. Reggio
Production Manager: Kathy Bontz

TFH Publications, Inc.®
One TFH Plaza
Third and Union Avenues
Neptune City, NJ 07753

Discovery Communications, Inc. Book Development Team: Marjorie Kaplan, President and General Manager, Animal Planet Media / Kelly Day, EVP and General Manager, Discovery Commerce / Elizabeth Bakacs, Vice President, Licensing and Creative / JP Stoops, Director, Licensing / Bridget Stoyko, Associate Art Director

Printed and bound in China

11 12 13 14 15 16   1 3 5 7 9 8 6 4 2

Library of Congress Cataloging-in-Publication Data
Lang, Laura, 1953-
   Cavalier King Charles spaniel / Laura Lang.
      p. cm.
   Includes bibliographical references and index.
   ISBN 978-0-7938-3715-1 (alk. paper)
   1. Cavalier King Charles spaniel. I. Title.
   SF429.C36L36 2011
   636.752'4--dc22
                                        2010052562

This book has been published with the intent to provide accurate and authoritative information in regard to the subject matter within. While every reasonable precaution has been taken in preparation of this book, the author and publisher expressly disclaim responsibility for any errors, omissions, or adverse effects arising from the use or application of the information contained herein. The techniques and suggestions are used at the reader's discretion and are not to be considered a substitute for veterinary care. If you suspect a medical problem consult your veterinarian.

Note: In the interest of concise writing, "he" is used when referring to puppies and dogs unless the text is specifically referring to females or males. "She" is used when referring to people. However, the information contained herein is equally applicable to both sexes.

The Leader In Responsible Animal Care for Over 50 Years!®
www.tfh.com

CONTENTS

1 ORIGINS OF YOUR CAVALIER KING CHARLES SPANIEL............4

2 CHARACTERISTICS OF YOUR CAVALIER KING CHARLES SPANIEL....14

3 SUPPLIES FOR YOUR CAVALIER KING CHARLES SPANIEL.........26

4 FEEDING YOUR CAVALIER KING CHARLES SPANIEL..............36

5 GROOMING YOUR CAVALIER KING CHARLES SPANIEL..........52

6 HEALTH OF YOUR CAVALIER KING CHARLES SPANIEL...........68

7 TRAINING YOUR CAVALIER KING CHARLES SPANIEL...........90

8 SOLVING PROBLEMS WITH YOUR CAVALIER KING CHARLES....108

9 ACTIVITIES WITH YOUR CAVALIER KING CHARLES SPANIEL.....120

RESOURCES......................................132

INDEX..138

ORIGINS OF YOUR CAVALIER KING CHARLES SPANIEL

There may be breeds that are a bit smarter, breeds that are better hunters, and breeds that are better guard dogs, but there may be no breed that is a better overall family companion than the Cavalier. Cavaliers are uncommonly affectionate as well as highly social and agreeable, and they have absolutely adorable looks to add to their list of pleasing qualities. It is no surprise that the Cavalier King Charles Spaniel is one of the most highly sought-after toy breeds in the world today.

EARLY DEVELOPMENT OF THE CAVALIER

No one is sure when the first toy spaniels came about, but it had to have been a very long time ago, as they have been depicted in paintings for hundreds of years. One of the earliest known of the tiny-type dogs was the original Maltese, known as *Canis melitaeus*, as long ago as 1000 BC. Much later a number of small reddish-and-white Oriental dogs were brought to Italy from the Middle East and at some point crossed with what was called *C. melitaeus*; the result was the appearance of the first little red-and-white spaniel-type dogs. Eventually some of these dogs were sent to France, where they became very popular.

DEVELOPMENT UNDER THE HOUSE OF STUART AND KING CHARLES II

Mary Queen of Scots always had some of these spaniels, even as a child, and as the famous story goes, one was found with her after she was executed in 1587. Mary was born Mary Stuart (aka Stewart) in Scotland and at the age of five went to France to live with Henry II. It was during her time in France that she more than likely acquired her love of the tiny spaniels who became part of the Stuart family. When Mary was old enough, she was married to Henry II's son, Francis II, who eventually became the king of France. After Francis's death, Mary returned to Scotland and married Lord Darnley, aka Henry Stuart. The union produced a son, King James VI of Scotland, who eventually became King James I of England. The emperor of Japan presented King James I with a gift of yet more of these spaniels. King Charles I was a son of King James I and father to King Charles II, and the spaniels continued to be part of the royal Stuart family.

When King Charles II came to the throne during the Restoration, his sister Henrietta brought some of her little spaniels from France to join the other tiny spaniels King Charles II already owned. The king adored his dogs and had them with him all the time—they were in attendance at all royal meetings, and he even allowed them to sleep and whelp puppies on his bed. Eventually these small spaniels became known as King Charles Spaniels. Some of the larger ones were

The Cavalier is uncommonly affectionate, highly social, and agreeable—the perfect family pet.

probably used for hunting, and even today many Cavaliers retain good hunting instincts. During this period the tiny spaniels were mostly red-and-white and black-and-white, although a tiny black spaniel was known to exist as well. It was not until the 19th century that the crossing of these tiny black spaniels with the Pyrame—an elegant little smooth-coated black-and-tan dog—brought about the black-and-tan toy spaniels. Later these black-and-tan dogs were crossed with a Miniature Toy Trawler to introduce the red gene that brought about the ruby-colored spaniel.

These tiny spaniels were kept mostly for warmth and to keep fleas off their humans—some even believed that they could prevent forms of stomach illnesses, but they were also considered a comfort to their owners. Hence these small spaniels were often called "spaniels gentle" or "comforters." Right from the beginning, many paintings depicted these small spaniels with their families and especially with children. There is little doubt that they held a special place in their families' hearts.

DEVELOPMENT UNDER WILLIAM OF ORANGE AND MARY

These toy spaniels continued to remain very popular, especially with the aristocracy, until the fall of the house of Stuart. William of Orange and his wife Mary came to the throne, and they preferred the Pug, so the toy spaniels went out of fashion and nearly disappeared. The larger hunting types remained, however, and those that were owned by John, 1st Duke of Marlborough, c. 1700, were referred to as the Marlborough Spaniel. It was during this time that the legend regarding the origin of the Blenheim (a red color) spot came about. While the duke was at battle, his duchess, Sarah, sat waiting for news of his safety. She had a spaniel bitch on her lap and continuously pressed her thumb on the bitch's head nervously. When the bitch whelped, all the puppies had a spot on the head the size of the Duchess's thumb. It is also said that a spaniel was with the duke at the Battle of Blenheim, which eventually gave rise to the name "Blenheim" for the red-and-white variety of spaniels.

During the reign of Queen Victoria, the Cavalier was bred to have a head similar to that of the Pekingese, pictured here.

DEVELOPMENT UNDER QUEEN VICTORIA

Although Queen Victoria grew up with a King Charles Spaniel named Dash and loved and promoted the breed, she was presented with the gift of a Pekingese while she was queen. Her gift happened to be one of the five famous Pekingese dogs who were found in the Summer Palace staying close to the bodies of their dead masters, who had killed themselves to avoid capture after the Allied occupation of Peking in 1860. The unique breed captured the heart of the queen and of the nation, and it wasn't long before people began to breed the King Charles Spaniels to have a shorter and shorter muzzle to look more like the Pekingese. Eventually, there were few left of the longer-muzzled King Charles Spaniels. During World War I, dog shows were shut down, and when they resumed, none of the longer-muzzled spaniels were left. Only the King Charles Spaniel, with its now flat face and domed head, was seen. This form of the breed continued to go on and still exists today as the King Charles Spaniel in the United Kingdom and the English Toy Spaniel in the United States.

RESURRECTION OF THE BREED

During the early 1920s, a wealthy American by the name of Roswell Eldridge came to England to purchase a pair of the longer-nosed spaniels as depicted in paintings he had seen at various galleries. He was surprised to find that there were none left to be seen. He preferred the old type of toy spaniel and decided to do something about it. Beginning in 1926, and for the next five years, he offered a prize of 25 pounds for the best dog and bitch at Crufts (an annual dog show hosted by England's Kennel Club) who most resembled those in the old paintings. A few breeders took him up on his offer and started breeding some of the King Charles Spaniel "cast-offs" who were thought to have too-long muzzles. Although it was obvious that some King Charles Spaniels reverted to having longer noses fairly easily, a lot of other mixing likely went on at the time—Papillons and English Cockers are two possible contributing breeds.

THE EVENTS OF 1928

Even though Eldridge did not live to see the results of his efforts, in 1928 the dog winner was Ann's Son. He was eventually chosen to set down the breed standard.

The first actual recorded Cavaliers came over to the United States from England in the early 1940s.

Ann's Son went on to a long show career, and by the time he retired, he had never been defeated.

In 1928 the Cavalier King Charles Spaniel Club (CKCSC) was founded by a small number of breeders at Crufts and the name for the "new" breed chosen. The dogs were often ridiculed but carried on, their numbers and quality slowly increasing.

POST-WORLD WAR II

After World War II, dog shows started up again and in 1945 the breed was recognized. In 1946, England's Kennel Club gave the breed its first Challenge Certificates. The first dog champion was Daywell Roger, whose dam, Daywell Nell, had

Historically, the real beginning of the breed in the United States was considered to be in 1952, when Mrs. Sally Lyons received her first puppy.

been sired by Ann's Son. The first bitch champion was a black-and-tan called Amanda Loo of Ttiweh. It was a slow start, but today the Cavalier greatly outnumbers the King Charles in registrations.

THE CAVALIER IN THE UNITED STATES

Although spaniel-type dogs were seen in paintings in the United States and there is one noted picture of a Cavalier with his family in the early 1900s, the first actual recorded Cavaliers came over from England in the early 1940s. These two older males, Robrull of Veren and Bertie of Rookerynook, were owned by Mrs. Harold Whitman and Mrs. John Schiff.

CREATION OF THE CAVALIER KING CHARLES SPANIEL CLUB, USA (CKCSC, USA)

The foundation and continued cultivation of the CKCSC, USA, the original breed club, can be credited to a few influential Cavalier owners.

The Influence of Sally Brown

Historically, the real beginning of the breed in the United States was considered to be in 1952 when Mrs. Sally Lyons Brown received her first puppy, a black-and-tan bitch named Psyche of Eyeworth. This puppy was a gift from her good friend Lady Mary Forward. Like most Cavalier owners, she was not satisfied with having just one and soon wanted more.

Because the Cavalier was not recognized by the American Kennel Club (AKC) at the time, there was no way to register Sally's dogs, so she sought out other Cavalier owners and in 1954 founded the Cavalier King Charles Spaniel Club, USA (CKCSC, USA). This became the original and only registering body for the breed for more than 40 years. Sally kept hard at work creating a studbook, incorporating the club in 1956, and also serving as the club's president until 1962.

The Influence of Trudy Brown

Sally's sister-in-law, Gertrude (Trudy) Polk Brown, eventually became known as the guardian of the breed in the United States. Trudy's first Cavalier came from Sally's bitch Mercury of Eyeworth. Eventually Sally turned the club over to Trudy. She continued to guide the club for many years and remained highly involved until her death in 1983. Several of the earlier shows were held on her property, and many longtime breeders today still remember attending shows at her estate.

The Influence of Elizabeth Spalding

Another one of the original influential people in the United States was Elizabeth Spalding and her Kilspindie dogs. Elizabeth was from Great Britain herself, and her first dogs were imports. Her Cavalier Pargeter Lotus of Kilspindie won Best in Show at the very first National Specialty in 1962. Her Pargeter Mermaid won Reserve Best in Show and Best of Opposite Sex at that same show. There were just 14 dogs and 21 bitches entered by 26 exhibitors, small as compared to today's standards.

THE BID FOR AKC RECOGNITION

The CKCSC applied to the AKC for Miscellaneous status early on, which was granted in 1962. It then attempted to gain full recognition several times but was rejected due to the small numbers of registered dogs. The club then decided to develop its own show system, and a stringent code of ethics was put in place to preserve the welfare of the breed.

Although many members did not participate in the AKC Miscellaneous Classes, several did participate in obedience. The first AKC Companion Dog obedience titles were gained in 1962 by Elizabeth Spalding with Miss Eda of Manscross, CD, and Kingfisher of Kilspindie, CD. The first AKC Utility Dog title was gained in 1976 by Katharine Foster with Shaggymeads Lord Chancellor, UD, and the second in 1979 by the author with a dog bred by Elizabeth Spalding, Kilspindie Lawmaker, UD. Since then many other Cavaliers and their owners have participated in performance events.

The club made as part of its by-laws a rule to poll the membership every five years as to whether to apply to the AKC for full recognition. Many breeders in the United States preferred to keep the breed protected under its strictly enforced stringent code of ethics but also recognized that

Over the years, the Cavalier's popularity has continued to rise.

some members might not agree and therefore kept this important decision to a democratic vote of all its members. By then the breed was becoming enormously popular in Great Britain because a Cavalier, Alansmere Aquarius, won Best in Show at Crufts in 1973. The members continued to vote down full recognition again and again by a huge margin, hoping that keeping the breed out of the AKC would preclude it from becoming hugely popular and commercially bred. The club kept its Miscellaneous Class status intact for the obedience participants.

The club happily went about its business for many years, growing steadily and adding more and more show weekends. Show participation grew by leaps and bounds, and it was not at all unusual to have well over 200 Cavaliers entered at most shows.

In 1992 the AKC decided that it was time to grant the Cavalier full recognition and invited the CKCSC to become the parent club for the breed. As required by the club by-laws, the vote had to be put to the entire membership once again. They voted overwhelmingly against recognition by a margin of nine to one! But things did not end there—the AKC was determined to add the Cavalier to its list of fully registered breeds.

A small group of Cavalier breeders from the CKCSC were afraid that another group of less experienced breeders would be recognized as the new AKC parent breed club, so it formed the American Cavalier King Charles Spaniel Club (ACKCSC) and applied to the AKC for parent club status. Eventually this was granted, and in 1995 the breed was officially recognized by the AKC. Cavaliers began competing for AKC championships in the Toy Group in January of 1996. The first Cavalier to successfully compete at Westminster was Ch. Partridge Wood Laughing Misdemeanor in 1996, garnering a Group placement. The ACKCSC held its first National Specialty in May of 1997.

THE CAVALIER KING CHARLES SPANIEL TODAY

The Cavalier has continued to rise steadily through the AKC ranks and is now the 25th most popular breed. Cavaliers compete in conformation, obedience, agility, and all other AKC venues and are quite competitive.

The original breed club in the United States, the CKCSC, continues to exist and thrive, keeping its strict code of ethics in place to protect the breed. It has always been careful to consider all of its members as equally important—whether they show, breed, or are simply happy to be the proud owner of one or more Cavaliers. Shows are still very well attended and run more like the English system, in which dogs have to compete against champions in the classes. This is different from the case in the United States, which separates champions into a separate Best of Breed class. You can find a lovely weekend of CKCSC specialties in various locations in the United States once every month throughout the year, giving its members a good excuse to attend several fun-filled mini-vacation weekends each year. Many of the attendees do not even show!

CHARACTERISTICS OF YOUR CAVALIER KING CHARLES SPANIEL

Would you like a dog to sit and cuddle with in the evening while you are relaxing or a dog who will gladly go on walks or even hiking with you in the woods? A dog who is intelligent and easy to train—either to become a delightful companion or to perform enthusiastically in the conformation, obedience, and/or agility ring? Or a dog who is totally comfortable either playing with children, helping you host a dinner party, or working in a therapy program at your local hospital or nursing home? How about a dog who will do all these things and more and look absolutely beautiful while doing it? That would be the Cavalier King Charles Spaniel!

PHYSICAL CHARACTERISTICS

The hallmarks of the Cavalier are his head and expression, with those large round eyes that are a very warm dark brown and have lots of cushioning around them. The cushioning around the eyes is what helps give them their soft and gentle expression, looking so sweet and somewhat like a stuffed animal. However, they are still a true spaniel under that angelic face and tend to have

The hallmark of the Cavalier is his head and soft, gentle expression.

an affectionate but quite sporting personality—despite their small package.

The Cavalier standard has been purposefully kept very similar among the various registries.

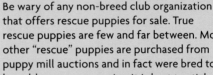

GENERAL BODY STRUCTURE

Cavaliers are a sturdy breed with a moderate amount of bone and body for their size. They should not be leggy and refined like an Italian Greyhound, for example. The body should be square when measured—about equal in height and length—but should give the appearance of being slightly longer than it is tall. This results from the breed's sturdy body proportions, having slightly more depth of body than similarly sized and proportioned breeds.

SIZE

The Cavalier's average height is about 12 to 13 inches (30.5 to 33 cm) at the top of the shoulders. Average weight is about 12 to 18 pounds (5.5 to 8 kg), leaning toward the heavier side. Cavaliers feel and are heavier than they look. It is rare to find a properly proportioned 13-inch-tall (33 cm) Cavalier who weighs only 18 pounds (8 kg). Most are closer to 20 pounds (9 kg). Cavaliers who weigh 12 pounds (5.5 kg) tend to be quite small—less than 11 inches (28 cm) in height.

Most of the "tiny" or "teacup" Cavaliers advertised are not any smaller in stature. They tend to be severely lacking in amount of bone and body and are much more fragile looking. This is *not* a good thing. They are more prone to skeletal problems, bone breakage, and other health issues. There are plenty of Cavaliers available from responsible breeders in the lower range for size and weight, so please do not purposefully search for a teacup size.

COAT

The Cavalier coat is supposed to be silky and straight, but a slight wave is permissible. The amount of coat can vary widely from very thin, flat, and short

to very thick, wavy, and long and everything in between. Neutering causes the growth cycle of the coat to lengthen and can cause the coat to be longer, fuzzier and wavier than it would have been. Excess weight also contributes significantly to a more profuse and woolly coat. Their coat is fairly short on top but has long feathering on the ears, tail, under the belly, legs and chest—very different from that of an American Cocker Spaniel. Professional grooming is not necessary in this breed, but it is perfectly okay to use a groomer if you want. An occasional bath, cutting of the nails once or twice a month, and regular brushing are all that is necessary. Cavaliers do shed pretty much all year round but in proportion to their small size. Brushing and combing the coat several times a week during shedding season will cut down on shedding tremendously.

COLORS

The Cavalier comes in four striking colors. There are two parti-color combinations, the Blenheim and the tricolor; and two whole-color combinations, the ruby and the black-and-tan. Markings can vary widely in parti-color Cavaliers, from very lightly marked (mostly white) to very heavily marked (mostly chestnut red or black). Some can be so lightly marked as to be missing the patch of color around one or both eyes. Many whole-colors have some white on them—some quite a bit of white. If you are looking for a pet, please do not let markings influence you in any way because they are nothing more than aesthetics. They don't affect the dog in any way, shape, or form—not in personality and not in health.

Blenheim

The Blenheim Cavalier should have rich chestnut red markings on a clear pearly white background. In an ideal world, a Cavalier should have an even amount of white versus chestnut red with the red well broken up in the white, but in reality they can vary from very heavily marked to very lightly marked, as previously mentioned. The red chestnut color can also vary in amount of richness from a paler, somewhat lemony color to a red that is almost brown in shade. The color will spread a bit as the puppy ages, so he will have more color as an adult than he did as an eight- to ten-week-old puppy. However, the red does not spread nearly as much as black does.

The head and ears should be chestnut red with a white blaze down the middle, fairly evenly divided, and a white muzzle. Some white blazes will have the red "Blenheim" spot in the center on the top of the head. This is a somewhat desired trait but far from being essential. Most champions do not have the Blenheim spot. Again, some Cavaliers may be missing red around one eye or both, but this does not affect the health of the dog in any way.

The white should be clear, without noticeable ticking—tiny spots of color in the white. These spots are also called freckles when seen on the head. Show dogs tend to be fairly clear because this is considered more striking and aesthetically pleasing, but again, it's a trait that doesn't affect the health of

The Cavalier comes in four striking colors: Blenheim (top left), tricolor (top right), black and tan (bottom left), and ruby (bottom right).

the dog in any way and so shouldn't negatively affect your choice of puppy. Most parti-color Cavaliers do have some ticking/freckling.

Tricolor

The tricolor Cavalier should have jet black markings on a clear, pearly white background with tan on the cheeks, underside of the ears, above the eyes, and under the tail, and if there's enough black on the body there may be some under the elbows, on the edges of the chest, or even on the legs. The head and ears should be black with a white blaze down the middle, fairly evenly divided, with a white muzzle.

The black-and-tan Cavalier has jet black coloring with tan markings.

Markings could range from very lightly marked to very heavily marked. Some tricolors are also born with the Blenheim spot, but the black tends to spread so much that it nearly always ends up as a bridge of black across the head instead of a spot. As a newborn puppy, there should be a fairly wide blaze. Narrower blazes nearly always fill in because of the tendency of the black to spread so much.

The white should be somewhat clear, with very little or no ticking.

Black and Tan

The black-and-tan Cavalier has jet black coloring with tan markings over the eyes, on the cheeks, on the underside of the ears, on the chest, under the tail, and on the legs. Some have varying amounts of white as well in the same spots as the ruby. (See below.) The black does spread a lot more than the red, and even amazing amounts of white in a black-and-tan puppy can disappear over time!

Ruby

The ruby Cavalier is a richly colored chestnut red all over. Some may have bits of white on top of their head (where the blaze would be on a Blenheim), on the muzzle or chin, on the chest, on the paws, or at the end of the tail. Some may even have more than a little bit. The red will spread somewhat so that tiny bits of white may well disappear as the puppy ages, with the chin, top of the muzzle, and center of the chest being the last to go.

LIVING WITH YOUR CAVALIER

The Cavalier is a small dog with a true spaniel temperament. Due to his long history of having been bred to be the ultimate companion/comforter spaniel, he has a truly wonderful temperament: somewhat active yet calm and empathetic to the max. He is often referred to as a big dog in a small dog package because he is neither as yappy nor as active as most other toy breeds. He possesses a fearless and sporting attitude yet is gentle and affectionate. The Cavalier is a truly loving and affectionate dog who seems to get along with everyone and everything—tail wagging the entire time!

ADAPTABILITY

Cavaliers are possibly the most adaptable of all breeds. When they are inside they act like a couch potato—they'll lie quietly with you for hours on the floor, on the couch, or in your lap. When they are outside they become a different dog and will be up for playing, retrieving, or going for a hike—and are very enthusiastic about it!

AFFECTIONATENESS

The Cavalier is a happy little dog who loves nearly everything and everyone. Cavaliers are very friendly with strangers, and this highly demonstrative breed absolutely loves to show affection. They are famous for their warm "hugs." (A hug occurs when you are sitting down and a Cavalier stands on your lap, puts one paw on each side of your neck, and leans in toward your face.) They will alternate this behavior with lots of licking kisses. If you lie on the floor they will give you more kisses and try to "smother" you with their body—often trying to lie right on top of your face!

Cavaliers just can't get enough from their owners. If you do not want a dog who follows you around, who always wants to lie on top of you or at least right next to you on the couch, or who wants to give you lots of hugs and kisses, the Cavalier is not the breed for you. Cavaliers thrive on being with their humans, and their need for affection is high, not far below that of a human child.

COMPANIONABILITY

Cavaliers thrive with companionship and are possibly the most highly social of all dog breeds. They seem healthier and happier and appear to live longer when they have the companionship of their human(s) and especially of another pet.

With Children

Cavaliers and children make a lovely combination. Did I mention that they make the best family pet? They are trustworthy, quiet but still playful, and highly tolerant. They don't seem to mind being dressed up in outfits by children or being pulled around in a wagon (under supervision of course) and yet love to play and retrieve with children. Most are so tolerant that they will accept even somewhat abusive behavior without a single grumble, so you need to watch to make sure that children—especially the younger ones who don't know any better—don't get overly rough with your dog.

With Other Pets

Most Cavaliers are submissive to other animals, so their ability to get along with any other pets you might have is very high. If there is a problem, it is rarely with the Cavalier. Just remember that they are spaniels underneath, so you might have

Cavaliers are trustworthy, playful, and highly tolerant of children.

Dog Tale

In recent years there was a television show called *It Takes a Thief*. It was a reality-type show that taught owners how best to protect their property from burglars. One episode took place at a residence with a black-and-tan Cavalier in attendance. While the crew was "burglarizing" the home, the Cavalier not only happily followed the "burglars" from room to room, but she also gladly went home with them. This was no surprise to owners of this friendly breed. Cavaliers do indeed love everyone—even burglars!

to take extra care if your other pet is a bird or rodent, as your dog's instincts can override training.

ENVIRONMENT

The Cavalier is quite possibly the most adaptable of all dogs. He does well in any environment—in the country, a high-rise in the city, or a typical house in the suburbs. He is just as happy sitting in your lap as he is hunting outside for birds and rabbits.

EXERCISE REQUIREMENTS

Cavaliers are a moderately active breed and should have no tendency toward being hyperactive. They don't need much additional exercise, as many breeds do, and will fare well with just two walks a day. They are athletic enough to go for a daily jog with their owner if it is at a moderate pace and not more than a few miles (km). If you jog at a fast pace or for more than 3 miles (5 km) a day, please do not take your Cavalier along. Never take a puppy. Wait until he is mature—fully grown with properly developed muscles—and start slowly. Also be sure that your Cavalier is sound enough by having his hips and patellae (knees) tested first. Some Cavaliers are just not sound enough to go jogging with you without doing structural damage.

GENDER

It is not true that the girls are sweeter, especially in this breed. In fact, the boys tend to be "more"—that is, they tend to show the personality traits of the Cavalier to a slightly greater extent. Cavaliers are a loving, affectionate, and highly demonstrative breed, so the boys tend to be even more so. Cavaliers can also be a somewhat dependent breed, and again, the boys may be even more so. Overall, the boys tend to be slightly better for active families or families with children, and

Cavaliers possess a high desire to please their owners.

the girls tend to be better for quieter people, singles, or retired people. However, remember that some boys will act like girls and some girls like boys—just as in humans—so it is best to go by the personality of any particular puppy you are interested in. Neutering tends to diminish these differences even more, so try to remain open-minded about which sex you would prefer.

HEALTH

Cavaliers, like *all* other breeds, have health problems—see Chapter 6 for more details.

Buy your Cavalier puppy from a responsible breeder only. A responsible breeder is one who is a member of the breed club and who tests her breeding stock for inheritable diseases to be able to make educated breeding choices to produce the healthiest puppies possible with the best temperaments. Responsible breeders sell all pets on restricted pedigrees, which prevents their dogs from being bred. Additionally, responsible breeders will take back your dog if you can no longer keep him. And finally, responsible breeders constantly socialize their puppies right from birth on so that they are best able to develop the temperament they were genetically born with. If you cannot see the mother of the puppy you are considering, cannot see pictures of the father at the very least, are not shown test results, or are being sold an unrestricted pet, you are probably not buying from a responsible breeder.

PROTECTION

The Cavalier is not a watchdog, and he is not a big barker either. Some will bark for a bit when excited by visitors but will usually settle down quickly. They will not only greet a burglar but follow him around the house and then go home with him.

TRAINABILITY

Cavaliers tend to be easy dogs to train. They are on the higher end of the intelligence scale, are very eager to learn, and have a high need to please their owners. Their biggest problem might be that they are small and overly cute, with such a sweet expression that they are given too much leniency right from the beginning. It is hard not to just "let it go" when a three-month-old Cavalier's puddle is so tiny and his antics so cute. Just one look at that angelic face and you can easily forget to be irritated. Many Cavaliers end up being spoiled because of this.

Like all other dogs, Cavaliers need something to do! They are smart enough to become bored if there is nothing to do and can get into considerable mischief. Keep your Cavalier's mind stimulated. Play games such as hiding things for him to find, or do some agility with him in your backyard. Your Cavalier will still enjoy it and you will have fun too!

Never forget that dogs are live animals. They are not inanimate objects with easily exchanged parts if they wear out early, and they are not easily disposed of should anything go wrong. If you want a healthy Cavalier, please buy from a responsible breeder and expect to pay a fair price. It costs money to produce healthy puppies with good temperaments. In the end you will probably end up spending less if you buy from a responsible breeder because your puppy will probably live longer and either have fewer health problems or have problems that are less severe in nature.

SUPPLIES FOR YOUR CAVALIER KING CHARLES SPANIEL

You have done your homework. You have researched the breed thoroughly and know that this is the breed for you. You have found a wonderful breeder who is knowledgeable and cares about the breed and raises puppies the way you want them to be raised. The breeder has a litter. You've met the puppies' mom and love her temperament. You have received proof that both parents of the litter were tested. And best of all, there is a puppy in that litter who seems to have been waiting just for you! In a few short weeks that puppy will be coming home to stay. Now it is time to get ready for the arrival of the new member of your family.

Below is a list of items you will need for your Cavalier. You can buy these items in a pet store or online. Purchasing supplies for your Cavalier can be a lot of fun, even though you are faced with a multitude of different choices!

BEDDING

There are many wonderful kinds of dog beds and bedding available today. Canvas sling beds, beds that look like miniature sofas, beds with thick cushions, soft and fluffy beds, cuddle balls, gel foam beds—there's a bed for every type of dog or problem that a dog may have. During your Cavalier's lifetime you will probably try them all! However, when you first bring your puppy home it is better to use old towels for bedding. There will almost certainly be potty

There are many great types of dog beds and bedding available today—and your Cavalier may even choose to nap on the couch!

mistakes, and it is better to have the puppy chew up or soil an old towel that can easily be washed or replaced than a beautiful new bed. That cute new puppy will grow up before you know it, and then you can try any or all of those fancy beds.

BE AWARE!
Never let your Cavalier ride loose in a moving car. Even in the mildest of fender benders he will become a hurtling missile and could get injured or worse.

CAR SEAT/CAR HARNESS/ CAR CRATE

Never let your Cavalier ride free inside your car when it is moving. He will become a hurtling missile in even the most minor fender bender and is likely to become injured or worse. It is much better to keep the furry member of your family safe—just as you do with your children.

You can use a crate to keep your puppy safe in the car or use a harness that is much like a seat belt, alone or in conjunction with a small car seat. A car seat can lift your Cavalier higher so that he can see outside the car while riding. For Cavaliers who might become carsick, sometimes just being able to see out the window can alleviate much of the motion sickness.

COLLAR

A buckle collar is the overall best choice, especially for a puppy. One that is 3/8 to 1/2 inch (1 to 1.25 cm) wide is good for a Cavalier-sized dog.

A large selection of nice colors and attractive designs are available today. Nylon is overall the best choice because it is very lightweight, strong, easily washable, and inexpensive. Leather is also a nice choice, but some can stain a dog's hair if the leash becomes wet. Stay away from a harness until your dog is completely trained not to pull. Used incorrectly, a harness can help create a dog who pulls instead of walking nicely with you.

CRATE

There are four basic kinds of crates on the market today.
1. folding (most of them are wire, but plastic ones are available as well)
2. plastic airline type
3. rattan/wicker type (these are made of a woven resin material similar to plastic)
4. cloth

CRATE MATERIALS

The traditional favorites are wire and plastic crates, and there are distinct advantages to both. Wire crates are great for very young puppies because you can easily keep a close watch on your puppy and see when he wakes up. They are also durable and last nearly forever with good care. It is harder to see inside plastic crates, but they are more den-like, and dogs seem to prefer them. They also have rounded corners and are less likely to damage car seats or the floors in your home. They are lighter and easier to transport from room to room or from house to car and back again. But both wire and plastic crates are good choices—many people will have one of each! They'll keep the wire enclosure in the living area for the daytime and a plastic enclosure in the bedroom for nighttime. They'll also use the plastic crate in the car when taking the dog to the vet or anywhere else.

Rattan and cloth crates can be nice looking and may make an attractive addition to your home, but stay away from them until your puppy is an adult. Both can be chewed up and/or chewed out of and peed on. Once your puppy is fully trained and past the chewing stage you may purchase one of these crates if you wish. The cloth enclosures are lightweight and portable. Both are nice to have, just not for a puppy.

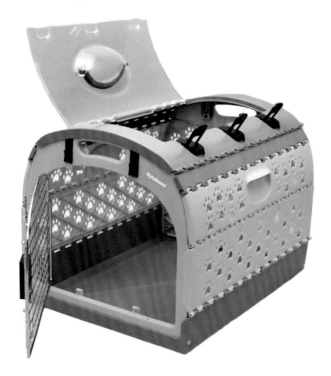

Traditionally popular crates include those made of wire and plastic, pictured here.

CRATE SIZE

For a Cavalier, the 200-size plastic crate is about right—or one that is about 18 to 20 inches wide (W) x 26 to 27 inches long (L) x 16 to 20 inches high (H) (45.5 to 51 x 66 to 68.5 x 40.5 to 51 cm). This is a good size for a puppy through an adult. If you decide to get a wire crate, one that is 18W x 24L x 20H (45.5 x 61 x 51 cm) is about right, or you may go a bit larger to the next size up, 21W X 30L X 24H (53.5 x 76 x 61 cm).

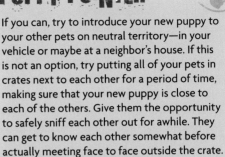

PUPPY POINTER

If you can, try to introduce your new puppy to your other pets on neutral territory—in your vehicle or maybe at a neighbor's house. If this is not an option, try putting all of your pets in crates next to each other for a period of time, making sure that your new puppy is close to each of the others. Give them the opportunity to safely sniff each other out for awhile. They can get to know each other somewhat before actually meeting face to face outside the crate. Believe that all will be fine. Dogs are great at reading body language—if your body language says it is okay, your dog will believe it.

If you decide to buy a wire or plastic enclosure, remember to buy the correct-sized divider panel with it. Use the divider panel to make the crate smaller when you first bring your puppy home. You want to make sure that he doesn't have enough room in his crate to pee in one end and curl up comfortably to sleep in the other end. Once your puppy is completely housetrained, the divider panel can be removed.

You can also buy a cloth cover for the wire crate to make it more like a den once your puppy is housetrained and past the chewing stage.

DOG FOOD

Buy a small bag of dog food for your puppy before you bring him home. A good choice for the first bag is the same food the breeder is feeding. If you cannot find the same food in your area, buy a good-quality food and make sure that the breeder gives you about a week's supply of the food the puppy is presently eating so that you can transition him to the new type. You might even ask the breeder to buy you a small bag to take home. See Chapter 4 for more information about choosing a quality food.

FENCING

Physical fencing is always the best for any dog and especially for the friendly Cavalier, who loves to visit everything and everyone. When you have physical fencing, no one—human, canine, or other animal—can get into your yard easily to hurt or take your dog. You don't have to fence the whole yard—just a small section will do. A 10-foot by 20-foot (3- by 6-m) section or even a little less is fine as a potty area, but there is not enough room to get decent exercise in, so you'll have to engage in more strenuous exercise elsewhere. The fence should be about 4 feet (2 m) high, but 3 feet (1 m) may be enough for most Cavaliers. They are intelligent and eager to please, so a fence to them usually means to stay inside. Although it is not common, there are some who will test the boundary and even a 4-foot (2-m) fence might not be enough. However, a 3- or 4-foot (1- or 2-m) fence is normally plenty except for the most determined of Cavaliers.

Some Cavaliers do dig now and then, but few are avid diggers. Keep an eye on your Cavalier as he matures to see whether he will be one who enjoys digging underneath or climbing over a fence. You may have to put something along the bottom of the fence to prevent him from digging underneath. Note that a single dog is usually fine—it's when you put two or more pets together that they are more likely to encourage each other to get into mischief. It becomes a competition of sorts.

FOOD AND WATER BOWLS

Food and water bowls are made with a variety of materials: stainless steel, glass/ceramic, and plastic. Stainless steel is a good choice because it will last forever with proper care and won't break. These bowls come in regular and nontip shapes. Glass or ceramic is also a good choice because they come in many attractive styles, colors, and patterns—although they can be broken. Avoid plastic

Stainless steel food and water bowls are durable and come in regular and nontip styles.

because it can be chewed and scratched, and cracks can harbor bacteria. Plastic bowls are just not as sanitary as the other bowl types.

Also available is what is called a spaniel bowl. These bowls are much narrower in diameter and taller, so as the dog drinks his ears fall to the outside of the bowl and don't get wet.

Another nice option is the crate dish—the hook-on or clamp-on type. This type can be attached to the inside of the crate so that your puppy has access to drinking water, with less chance of upsetting the bowl, while inside the enclosure. This is great for when you aren't at home and your puppy needs to stay inside the crate for any length of time.

GATE

Many types of gates are available. Some are completely portable, some need to be permanently attached to the wall, and others use pressure to stay in place. Gates are another way to keep a dog in an area or out of an area.

GROOMING SUPPLIES

You will need brushes, combs, nail clippers, scissors, toothpaste and a toothbrush, and shampoo and conditioner. See Chapter 5 for a detailed list and explanation of what you need to purchase and for information on how to groom your Cavalier.

IDENTIFICATION

It's a good idea to purchase an ID tag for your puppy. If he should ever escape your yard, whoever finds him will be able to contact you quickly.

In addition to an ID tag, an implanted microchip is a vital means of identification because it can never get lost the way a collar and tags can. The chip is inserted under the skin in a similar way to how a vaccination is given, except the needle used to insert the chip is larger. The microchip is about the size of a small grain of rice and has a number embedded inside it. Once your dog has a microchip implanted, register his number with the national registry. The number can be read by a scanner; nearly all vets have a scanner and just about all dog shelters have one. All dogs taken to a shelter are scanned immediately to see whether they have a chip. If for any reason your Cavalier ends up in a shelter that does not have a no-kill policy, he is highly unlikely to be euthanized until all options have been exhausted if he has a microchip.

LEASH

You can buy leashes in a 4-foot or 6-foot (1 or 2 m) length; some come in other lengths too, both shorter and longer. A taller person might prefer a 6-foot (2-m) lead, whereas a shorter person might prefer a 4-foot (1-m) lead. For around-the-house training, the lightest-weight collar and lead that you can find is best. You want it to be easy for a tiny 12-week-old puppy to drag around and short enough that it is less likely to get tangled around furniture.

A nylon leash that matches the collar is a good choice. Leather is also appropriate, especially if you choose a leather buckle collar. Many people prefer the retractable leashes because they can be used at both shorter and longer lengths, but they aren't the best for training or for walking in a busy environment, such as a hectic street. Stay away from chain leashes; they are too heavy for a Cavalier.

A nylon leash is a good choice for walking your Cavalier.

Cavaliers enjoy a variety of toys, especially if they're fuzzy.

TOYS

Cavaliers seem to love fuzzy toys but for different reasons. Some love to carry them around as a favorite possession, while others delight in "killing" the toy as quickly as possible (chewing the squeaker out) and removing the "innards" (the stuffing inside), leaving just the "carcass" (the cloth the toy was covered with) to carry about. Always keep an eye on your Cavalier whenever he has access to a fuzzy toy to make sure that he doesn't eat the stuffing. Cavaliers also enjoy sturdy rubber toys that can be stuffed with kibble, treats, or peanut butter. Many love balls and/or Frisbees as well.

Some Cavaliers will play with toys by themselves, while others will need a buddy to play with. They are good retrievers on the whole, but not all of them will retrieve.

X-PEN

An "x-pen" is short for "exercise pen." It is a portable fence made of wire, mesh, or fabric that can be used to contain a dog to a certain area or to keep him out of an area and can be used both inside and outside the house. An x-pen is useful during housetraining or to minimize chewing and getting into other mischief, such as unrolling toilet paper all over your home—a favorite pastime for some Cavaliers.

FEEDING YOUR CAVALIER KING CHARLES SPANIEL

F ood provides two major functions. The first is to provide the nutrients
needed to produce new cells for both growth and repair; the second is to
provide energy so that we may breathe, digest, think, and move about. In
essence, every function takes energy, and that energy must be supplied by food.
The right amount of food and the right balance are as important to dogs as they
are to us, yet a dog's needs are different from a human's. This chapter will help
you understand how best to feed your Cavalier.

THE DOG'S DIGESTIVE SYSTEM

The dog's digestive system is quite different from the human digestive system. It is
much shorter and built to utilize animal protein more efficiently, so dogs require a
higher percentage of protein than humans do. Carbohydrates play a lesser role in
their diet. However, there is one way that dogs are quite similar to us. Dogs have
an immune system and can develop an illness, cancer, or other chronic condition
just as we humans can. This means that real, whole food is just as important to
a dog's health as it is to humans. Unfortunately, fewer studies have been carried
out with real whole-food diets than have been with commercially prepared kibble
diets, so it is still a bit riskier to feed a homemade cooked or raw diet. All other

The right amount
of food and the
right balance are as
important to dogs as
they are to humans.

things being equal, a fresh whole-foods diet is almost certainly healthier for a dog than many of the highly processed foods that are the most popular way to feed a dog today.

Cavaliers are on the smaller side and have less ability to store nutrients, so shortages are likely to show up in them sooner. Until enough studies have been done it is probably best to stick to commercially prepared diets with some whole-food meals added or to seek professional help with regard to preparing your dog's homemade diet.

WHAT IS A BALANCED DIET?

A balanced diet is one that contains the proper amounts and percentages of carbohydrates, fats, and proteins, along with the proper amounts and percentages of necessary vitamins and minerals that will lead to the healthiest possible Cavalier.

CARBOHYDRATES

Carbohydrates are basically sugars—both simple and complex—and provide energy to the body. Simple carbohydrates convert easily to sugar and provide quick energy. Complex carbohydrates take longer to digest and absorb because the units of sugar must be separated from the chain before absorption can take place. Good sources of carbohydrates are fruits, vegetables, and grains.

Dogs are capable of utilizing both proteins and carbohydrates for energy, so their actual need for carbohydrates is low, which is why most dogs in the wild eat a diet that comprises only about 10 percent carbohydrates. However, it is much cheaper for dog food manufacturers to use carbohydrates in their food to supply energy, so you will find that most dry kibbles are made up of 30 to 70 percent carbohydrates. There is nothing wrong with a very low percentage of carbohydrates as long as the balance is made up of quality proteins. If you would like to know what percentage of carbohydrates your dog food contains, just look at the various percentages shown on the package (protein, fat, fiber, etc.), add them all up, and subtract from 100. The remainder is the percentage of carbohydrates in that particular food.

FATS

Dietary fatty acids are critical for growth, reproduction, and maintenance of a healthy skin and coat. Good sources include most vegetables, nuts, seeds, and fish oils. Cavaliers seem to need a food with about 14 percent fat content to keep their coats in optimal shape. Scientists are also finding that essential fatty acids

Fats in the diet are critical for the maintenance of a healthy skin and coat.

such as omega-3s and -6s are as important for dogs as they are for humans, and many kibbles have already added them.

Note that excess fats also play a role in disease. Some fatty acids resemble bacterial invaders, causing the immune system to attack them and cause inflammation. This is one reason why it's necessary to limit the percentage of fat your Cavalier consumes.

PROTEINS

Proteins contain essential amino acids, which are the building blocks for growth and repair of the body. Good sources of high-quality, easily digestible proteins for dogs can be found in meats such as chicken, beef, and lamb, but you should substitute others such as venison, rabbit, or salmon now and then. *Dry* dog food should contain at least 22 percent protein, as this is the minimum dogs require for basic maintenance. The more water a food contains, the lower the protein percentage will be.

VITAMINS AND MINERALS

Vitamins and minerals are the other essential elements required in the diet eaten by living organisms. They boost the immune system, support normal growth and development, and help cells and organs do their jobs. Vitamins are organic—that is, made by plants and animals—whereas minerals are inorganic and come from the soil and water. The majority of chemical names you see in the ingredient list of any commercial dog food are the added vitamins and minerals.

WATER

Mammals are composed mostly of water, a nutrient that is essential for life. Water is necessary to keep the body properly hydrated for everything to keep working properly. Dogs are always losing water through perspiration and urination, and that water must be continuously replaced. Keep a bowl of cool, clean water out for your Cavalier at all times unless otherwise advised by your veterinarian. It does not help to deprive a puppy or aging dog of water to help prevent potty accidents in the middle of night. In fact, I believe that it is better to have water available to your Cavalier even when he is inside his crate. I keep a filled water bowl in my dogs' crates—one that hangs from the side.

COMMERCIAL DIETS

Commercial diets are the most popular diets due to ease of use, the fact that most are balanced to American Association of Feed Control Officials (AAFCO) guidelines, and the fact that they are cost efficient.

When feeding a commercial diet, it is a good idea to start with what the breeder is feeding and then change it as you wish. Note that dogs are no different from humans—they have no more trouble changing diets than we do. The problem is that we tend to feed the exact same food every single meal for months and even years. If you were to eat the exact same thing for every single meal for a year, you would have the same problem with an abrupt change in diet as our dogs do. If you want to avoid this problem, change your dog's diet frequently. Buy the smallest amounts possible of multiple types of foods and feed some of this and some of that, changing every few days or so. Changing foods may help reduce any deficiencies a particular food may have due to its makeup or the way your dog utilizes what he is eating.

PUPPY POINTER

Don't worry if your puppy is a picky eater. No matter how picky he is now, there will come a day that you will wish your gluttonous Cavalier was picky again!

DRY FOOD (KIBBLE)

Manufacturers began making dry dog food during World War II from the "scraps" left of what was not used for human food. Today dry food is the easiest to

Kibble may offer some cleaning benefit to the teeth due to its abrasive action when chewed.

feed, easiest to store, can be safely stored for some time, and is inexpensive to use, making it the most popular way to feed. Dry foods are getting better and better in quality but are still a highly processed form of diet.

Kibble may offer some chewing exercise and also some cleaning benefit to the teeth because of the abrasive action of the kibble when chewed. However, because of the way dogs naturally eat, most will swallow the food whole, especially those kibbles made with smaller pieces, so there is often no benefit to the teeth. If you want your Cavalier to acquire some of this benefit, you may need to buy a larger-sized and/or harder kibble.

Most of today's kibbles are preserved with natural preservatives such as vitamin C even though they can go bad more quickly, so buy smaller bags if possible. You might even check into sharing with friends, neighbors, and family—each can buy a different kind and give all of the dogs a variety.

How to Pick a Good Kibble

Once you read these short paragraphs over you will realize that you know a lot more about picking a good kibble than you thought! Common sense truly prevails here.

- A quality food should contain superior sources of protein, either whole fresh meats or a single-source meat meal, e.g., chicken meal rather than a generic-sounding "poultry" meal. It should also contain this whole-meat source as one of the first two ingredients. Whole, unprocessed grains should be used as well as fruits and vegetables, but don't go overboard looking for fruits and vegetables to be high up on the list of ingredients in a highly processed dry kibble. Because of the way in which kibble is processed, the majority of nutrients in fruits and vegetables are processed right out of the food. It is better to include small amounts of whole, raw, unprocessed fruits and vegetables in your dog's diet instead.

- A quality dry food should contain very little to none of the following ingredients: food fragments and meat by-products. Food fragments are lower-cost by-products of another food manufacturing process and include ingredients such as brewer's rice and wheat bran. The inclusion of these poor ingredients is only to help bring down the cost of the food. Any food that contains meat by-products as the major protein source is a low-quality product.
- A quality dry food should never contain fats or proteins named generically (e.g., animal fat or poultry fat instead of beef fat or chicken fat); artificial preservatives such as BHA, BHT, or ethoxyquin; artificial colors; or sweeteners such as corn syrup, sucrose, ammoniated glycyrrhizin, or propylene glycol.

CANNED

Canned food is more expensive than kibble but not as expensive as raw food. Again, some canned foods may contain poor ingredients, so be careful. Many

canned dog foods smell great to a dog, and some smell good enough for you to want to take a taste. Few dogs will refuse canned food, so it can be a good alternative for a dog who is ill and has little appetite. You need to feed a lot more canned food to get the same number of calories into your dog because so much water is added.

SEMI-MOIST

This type of food tends to taste better to dogs and is more expensive than kibble. In general, the ingredients used are not as good, and most add propylene glycol to make them "chewy"—not such a good ingredient to feed a dog. There tends to be more added sugar and

Canned food can be a good option for a dog who is ill and has little appetite.

flours too. A semi-moist food might be nice as a special meal now and then but is not the best food for every day.

COMMERCIAL RAW

A commercially prepared raw food diet is one that is prepared with raw ingredients by an outside manufacturer who then sells it to the public. Some are even made to AAFCO standards. This type of diet is also quite convenient but the most expensive way to feed. It is probably well worth the money, however, because it may be one of the healthiest options for your dog available today.

Again, some commercial raw diets are made with bad ingredients, so be careful. If you don't want to use commercial raw food regularly, consider feeding it as a special meal now and then—or even better, once or twice a week. Remember that raw has to be kept frozen until it is used, and once thawed, has to be kept in a refrigerator until the remainder is used. You also have to use the thawed remainder within a limited number of days.

NONCOMMERCIAL DIETS

A noncommercial diet is food that is prepared at home, mixing together a variety of separate ingredients—from a store, a farm, your own property, or elsewhere.

A healthy diet will keep your dog looking and feeling his best.

This is the same as preparing a meal from scratch for yourself and/or your family. A noncommercial diet can be fed raw or cooked.

HOME-COOKED DIET

There are lots of good books and e-mail lists to help you should you desire to cook your dog's food. One advantage of a home-cooked diet is that you know exactly what is in the food. You can also control which ingredients are used in each meal, as well as the quality of the ingredients. Some disadvantages of a home-cooked diet include the fact that it is more expensive and time consuming, and it may be hard to make sure that it is fully balanced. You will probably have to add a vitamin/mineral supplement when feeding this type of diet—check with your vet.

BONES AND RAW FOOD (BARF) DIET

Also known as the Biologically Appropriate Raw Food diet, a bones and raw food diet is similar in cost to a home-cooked diet but is not as expensive as a commercially prepared raw food diet. The BARF diet is easily digested and works well for dogs with allergies. You can also control the quality of the ingredients, as well as what is in the food. However, a raw diet is expensive, difficult to balance, takes a lot of time to prepare, is messy to prepare and feed, and can contain harmful bacteria. Dogs are not as susceptible to *E. coli* as humans are because their digestive system is so different, but they are more susceptible to *Salmonella* from raw chicken. You must be very careful to wash preparation areas and your hands well every time you prepare your dog's food because as rarely as it happens, there is still some possibility of passing a bacterial infection from a BARF diet to children or adult humans. Check with your vet before embarking on a raw food diet to be sure that you are planning to do everything correctly.

DIET ADDITIONS

Some common diet additions include supplements, vegetables, scraps, and treats.

SUPPLEMENTS

Dry food is produced by either extrusion or baking. During the extrusion process, a mixture of raw materials is fed into an expander, while pressurized steam or hot water is added. It is cooked at a high temperature for many

BE AWARE!
Unless you have a very active or sick adult Cavalier, it is better to feed just one meal a day. Twice-a-day feedings tend to create obese Cavaliers.

hours and allowed to dry. Because of this, most vitamins and minerals and other nutrients that are not heat tolerant are lost. That is why dog food companies add vitamins, minerals, and oil back into their food—they literally spray it on the kibble at the end. (This is like taking a Thanksgiving dinner and cooking it to death but then adding a vitamin/mineral supplement to the meal to make sure that we get what we need.) Therefore, dogs do not generally need supplements unless they are sick or have a chronic medical problem. Check with your vet before feeding any supplements.

VEGETABLES

I strongly suggest giving your dog some vegetables at least a couple of times a week and up to once a day. Dogs need their antioxidants just as we do. Feed vegetables as a treat—dogs seem more eager to eat any item they perceive as a treat. Give your dog whatever vegetable you are eating that day. Only a teaspoon or so each time is needed for a dog the size of a Cavalier.

Stick to tiny treats when training, like a piece of kibble or even a small piece of veggie.

Many Cavaliers are true gluttons who love to eat!

SCRAPS

Technically there is nothing wrong with feeding scraps, but if you feed your Cavalier too many, it may throw his diet out of balance. Also, some scraps contain too much added sugar, salt, and/or fat and may add empty calories to his diet. When feeding a scrap now and then, be sure that the item isn't toxic to dogs. You can find toxic food listings online.

TREATS

Stick to tiny treats—a very small-sized treat or even pieces of kibble— for training. For other treats, nothing is better than real food! Why not give your Cavalier a baby carrot or a strawberry or two instead of a grain-based treat? Other good treats include raw marrow bones or any type of treat that will enable your dog to chew safely for extended periods, giving him chewing exercise and helping clean his teeth.

FEEDING SCHEDULE

Dogs are not like humans—they don't need three square meals a day. Dogs in the wild are more equipped to gorge themselves in one sitting and then go for days without eating. Puppies from 9 to 12 weeks can be fed three small meals a day. From 12 weeks to 6 months, two medium-sized meals are plenty. Somewhere around seven to eight months you may change to a once-a-day feeding schedule.

I do not suggest feeding adult toy dogs more than once a day unless they are unusually active, have digestive problems, or are sick. The reason is that toy dogs as a rule eat very small amounts of food. Trying to divide a very small meal into two much smaller-sized meals is a recipe for disaster. Most humans will look at that 1/4 cup (57.5 g) or less of food and find it an impossibly small amount. Then they just can't help but add a tiny bit "extra" to each meal. Over time this tiny bit adds up to a lot of extra pounds (kg) on your Cavalier and leads directly to obesity. In my many years in this breed I have found only a tiny percentage of pet Cavaliers in good weight—most are at least 5 pounds (2.5 kg) overweight. In a breed prone to heart problems, this can literally be a death sentence.

I also do not suggest free feeding, leaving food out all day for a dog. From my experience it tends to produce poor eaters on the whole. It teaches dogs to eat slowly and pick at their food. It is not a good idea to keep food sitting out all the time either—it could spoil. I suggest feeding on a schedule, leaving the food bowl out for a certain amount of time and then picking it up until the next meal.

HOW MUCH TO FEED

Cavaliers, like all other breeds, can vary quite astonishingly in the amount of food they need to eat on a daily basis. It depends on the dog's size, activity level, metabolism, and many other things. Most Cavaliers tend to be "easy keepers" in that they need 1/2 cup (115 g) or less of a good-quality kibble per day, but other Cavaliers may need a full cup (230 g) or more each day. Puppies usually need about 1/4 to 1/3 cup (57.5 to 76 g) of food at each meal at 8 to 16 weeks of age, which can increase to 1/2 cup (115 g) or more at each meal when in a growth spurt. Most go through a major growth spurt after they reach four months of age and another minor growth spurt after they reach seven months of age. Boys will go through these spurts a bit later than the girls, and some boys may have an additional growth spurt at about 10 to 12 months of age. Many will suddenly quit eating after eight months of age, consuming so little that their owners become concerned. But at this point they have

Dog Tale

Often the same owner who calls to say that she has changed foods several times and her puppy doesn't like anything is also the same one who calls to ask how to stop her puppy from eating everything else—sticks, toilet paper, bugs, plants, even his own waste. The lesson to be learned is that dogs are not that picky! It isn't that your puppy doesn't like his food—he is just learning how to get what he wants.

An overweight Cavalier likely needs more exercise and less food.

completed the majority of their growing and don't need as much food—so don't worry if your Cavalier does this. (Some never go through this stage, however.)

Be careful—Cavaliers are small dogs. No matter how thin or lacking in appetite your puppy may be, he is almost sure to end up a good eater at some later point. It is the rare puppy who actually eats so little food that he starves himself to death.

FOOD ALLERGIES

If your Cavalier develops a food allergy, it may be to protein. Other allergies can be to grains; corn and wheat are common, but a particular dog, just like a human, can be allergic to just about anything. If your Cavalier develops a food allergy, first try buying a better-quality food if you don't already feed one. Next change the protein source. If you have been feeding a food based on chicken, change to lamb or fish. If eating beef, change to chicken or lamb. (Note that some dogs can manifest allergies as an ear infection. I know of a dog who got ear infections only when fed beef; once beef was eliminated from her diet, she never got another ear infection.) You can also try the elimination diet, where you feed just one ingredient for a while and see whether the dog reacts, and if not, add one more item to his diet every week or so, waiting to see whether there is a reaction. Once there is a reaction, you will then know which food is the culprit and can eliminate that food completely from his diet.

If you can't find the source of the allergy, you may need to contact your vet or a nutrition specialist.

OBESITY

How can you tell whether your Cavalier is overweight? Your vet is not necessarily the best person to ask! Over the years I have been surprised to find that many vets are reluctant to tell an owner that a dog is overweight until the dog becomes obese.

PERFORM THE RIB AND WAIST TESTS

Here are two ways to judge whether your Cavalier is overweight.

Rib Test

First is the rib test. Look for a hand or dish towel and fold it in half. Find a wire crate or wire fencing, something with wire spaced not more than 2 inches (5 cm) apart. Rub the towel over the wire several times and get used to how it feels.

The right amount of exercise will help your Cavalier maintain a healthy weight.

How does the wire feel—how easily does the towel move under your fingers? Now rub your fingers over your dog's ribs. He should feel somewhat similar—a thin amount of skin that moves easily over his ribs—ribs that can easily be felt and counted. If you feel some padding under the skin, he is mildly overweight. If you feel a lot of padding and have to press a bit to feel individual ribs and the skin doesn't move around easily, he is overweight. If you can't feel his ribs at all, he is seriously overweight.

Waist Test

The second test is the waist test. Stand over the top of your dog and look down at him while he is standing—he should be facing the same direction you are. You can also use your hands with this test. As you are looking down at your dog, look to see where his ribs are. If you are not sure, run your hands from his shoulders, over his ribs, and down to where his ribs end so that you know just where they are. After the last rib and before the hindquarters, you should see a distinct indentation: a waist. If you can barely see an indentation, your dog is mildly overweight. If there is no indentation at all, he is seriously overweight.

CUT BACK ON FOOD

You may be wondering exactly how to cut back on food. First you need to believe that if your dog is gaining weight, he is getting enough food. No ifs, ands, or buts about it. No matter how much you cut back on his food, if he is still gaining weight, he is still eating too much!

If this is the case with your dog, consult with your vet to decide by how much you should reduce his daily food ration. If you are feeding kibble, one way to give your dog less but still make him feel full is to soak half of his meal in water long enough that it expands. Mix the other dry half in with the expanded wet food. The expanded food will help your dog feel a bit fuller after eating. Then add some green beans—fresh or thawed frozen (canned tends to have too much salt)—to the top and feed. The green beans are a low-calorie filler and quite good for your dog too!

EXERCISE YOUR DOG MORE

Try to take your Cavalier for a daily walk, especially if you don't normally do so. The exercise will be good for you too. If you can't do that for whatever reason, attempt to play fetch with him for 15 minutes a day. Or tether your dog to you while you are working around the house so that he has to walk around with you instead of sleeping on the couch. Or throw some of his kibble meal so that he has to go and fetch it—you can even throw his entire meal one piece at a time.

GROOMING YOUR CAVALIER KING CHARLES SPANIEL

Cavaliers are a long-feathered breed with shorter hair on top and feathering on their ears, chest, legs, tail, and abdomen. Their hair can knot and pull on the skin, so they must be groomed regularly to keep them feeling comfortable. Grooming time is also a good time to check your dog over for other problems such as the teeth to see whether they are getting more dirty than a good brushing can handle; the skin to check for lumps, bumps, and scrapes; the ears to see whether there is any excess buildup of dirt or wax; the eyes to see whether there are any ulcers or scratches; and so on.

And don't forget, grooming feels good too! When you get to the final brushing stage, do it in such a way that it feels like a massage. This is a good way to bond with your dog, and he will love you for it!

GROOMING SUPPLIES

The Cavalier is considered a natural breed. This means that he has an easy-care coat and should not have to go to a groomer periodically to get his hair clipped or stripped as many breeds such as the Poodle do. You will only need a few items to groom your Cavalier properly.

COMBS

You will need at least two different types of combs. The first should be a metal comb with fine or medium-spaced teeth or a combination of the two. This is a

A natural bristle brush will smooth out and bring a shine to the coat.

good comb with which to begin your grooming routine—it helps tease out tangles.
The other comb you will need is a flea comb. This comb has closely spaced teeth and is great for pulling out dead hair when your Cavalier is shedding. It can be used after he is almost totally groomed and just before the final brushout with the natural bristle brush. And of course it can be used also to separate fleas from the skin!

FLAT NATURAL BRISTLE BRUSH
This is a very soft, natural bristle brush that is cut totally flat across the top. It is great for the final step in grooming because it will smooth out and bring a shine to the coat. Cavaliers *love* this part of their grooming routine because it feels so good.

SLICKER BRUSH
A slicker brush has a handle and a flat plastic head with bent metal pins embedded into it. Buy a well-made one with flexible and rounded pins so that it is less likely to hurt your Cavalier. The slicker is good for brushing the ears, tail, and other feathering on your dog.

PIN BRUSH
A pin brush has a number of straight, rounded metal "pins" embedded into it. This is a good brush to use while blow-drying your Cavalier because the space between the pins seems to do a good job separating the hair and allows for a quicker drying time.

STRIPPING KNIFE (OPTIONAL FOR NEUTERED DOGS)
Use a stripping knife to remove excess hair from your spayed or neutered Cavalier. Neutered Cavaliers have a longer hair growth cycle and tend to grow a more profuse coat, so you may want to do a bit of stripping to keep your dog looking sleeker. Cavaliers who have not been neutered do not tend to get that much coat and rarely need to be stripped—and the standard declares that show dogs are not to be stripped.

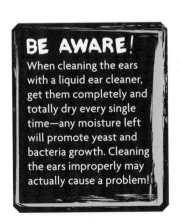

BE AWARE!
When cleaning the ears with a liquid ear cleaner, get them completely and totally dry every single time—any moisture left will promote yeast and bacteria growth. Cleaning the ears improperly may actually cause a problem!

SCISSORS

Scissors are used in two different ways. The first is to cut the hair between the pads on the bottom of the feet. Failure to do so can cause the hair to grow long and mat. I have groomed Cavaliers whose pads were completely hidden underneath a mass of matted hair because their owners failed to do this. The poor dogs were literally walking on a ball of matted hair—ouch!

The other use is to help cut out tangles. Most tangles can be teased out with your fingers, but sometimes you'll need more and the scissors will help.

NAIL CLIPPERS

Clippers are used to keep the Cavalier's nails short. A few different types of clippers exist. For most people, the easiest to use is the scissors type, while the safest to use is the guillotine type **because** it has a built-in stop, so you cannot cut too much at a time. Alternatively, you can also use a grinder to grind the nails down. With a grinder the nails can be safely made a bit shorter and will also be left with a smooth surface. A grinder may not be easy to use with a longhaired dog because the hair can get caught in the grinding mechanism if you are not careful, but when used correctly, it can result in a beautifully "cut" nail with no sharp edges. Once you become an expert at using the grinder, it

Clipping your Cavalier's nails is an important part of the grooming process.

A grooming table may make it easier to groom your dog.

will be much quicker to keep the nails short and smooth.

GROOMING TABLE OR SURFACE

You can purchase an actual grooming table, or buy a rug with skid-proof backing and put it on any raised surface to use as a grooming area.

COAT CARE

Most Cavaliers need to be groomed about once a week. During shedding season you may need to increase this to twice a week for a few weeks. Grooming should be done on a raised surface—either a grooming table or on a rug with skid-proof backing on some raised surface. Pick up your Cavalier and put him on your surface of choice.

BRUSHING

Gather your brushing supplies. You'll need the wider-spaced comb, slicker brush, bristle brush, and possibly the scissors and flea comb. Your Cavalier will need to be brushed just once a week unless it's shedding season, as previously mentioned.

How to Do It

Begin with the wider-spaced comb and comb all over, looking for knots. Popular places to find knots are behind the ears, under the elbows, at the loins (behind the ribs and just before the hind legs), the back of the hindquarters, and sometimes the neck and chest area. If you find a knot, try to carefully comb it out. You can spray the coat with a detangler to help as well, and sometimes you can use your fingers to tease the knot out. If all else fails, try cutting the knot with scissors. Cut in the same direction the hair goes—right down the center of the knot. Sometimes this is all that is needed and the rest of the knot will comb out easily. Occasionally you may have to cut more than once.

After you have finished combing out all the knots, use the slicker brush to comb him all over gently—those tiny pins can hurt!—and especially on all the feathering on the ears, legs, chest, tail, hindquarters, and under the belly.

If it is shedding season, comb your dog a few more times with the flea comb. It does a great job of pulling out the dead hair and can speed up the shedding process, minimizing the amount of hair left on your furniture or clothing.

Last, go over your dog well using the soft natural-bristle brush. Take your time with the brush because dogs enjoy this part the best. If you do it correctly, it will feel just like a soothing massage to your pet. It will also bring out the shine in the coat by redistributing the coat's natural oils.

After you've removed your Cavalier's drying coat, lightly brush him out.

Note: If you always find tangles in a particular area, try to find a reason. If there are nearly always knots behind the ears, for example, there may be an ear infection going on that's causing your dog to scratch the area, leading to more tangling. If you find tangles in the loin or underbelly area, he may be licking that area a lot for some reason. If you find them in the chest and neck area, it may be that your dog is drooling when anxious. These areas may need to be attended to more often or in a different way.

BATHING

Bathe your Cavalier whenever he is dirty. This can be once a week for highly active Cavaliers who spend a lot of time outside or for those who are shown, or as little as once every three months for true couch potatoes. If you use the right shampoo and conditioner and the dog is getting proper nutrition with enough fat, bathing will not dry out his coat. But use a doggy shampoo because it has the right pH for dogs; a human shampoo does not. There are lots of good shampoos on the market.

For Cavaliers with white on the coat, consider using a shampoo with optical brighteners to make the white appear even whiter. For those dogs with black or chestnut red, special shampoos are available to brighten those colors.

You can bathe your Cavalier in your tub, a laundry tub, or even the kitchen sink if it is large enough. It is helpful to have a spray hose but not necessary. A cup will do nicely to wet down and rinse your dog's hair. I use a laundry tub, purchased a stainless washer fill hose, and put a sprayer on the end of it. This works great for me!

How to Do It

Put your Cavalier into the tub and soak him down. Put your doggy shampoo of choice on each part of your dog and gently work the shampoo into the coat, shampooing the dirtier parts longer. When done I shampoo the whole dog all over again, making the experience as enjoyable as possible. This helps with those dogs who do not like getting wet. I do the ears last. You can use a doggy shampoo but you will find that many show people use dishwashing detergent instead on the ears. It seems to do a better job. Next rinse your dog really, really well, making sure that all traces of shampoo are washed away. Finally I apply conditioner to the back and sides of the dog and leave for a few minutes, then thoroughly rinse the coat once again.

Bathe your Cavalier whenever he is dirty—this can be once a week for highly active dogs who spend a lot of time outside.

After bathing, dry your dog as thoroughly as you can with a towel.

Dry your dog as thoroughly as you can with a towel and then comb him out. You can let him drip-dry, or you might want to blow-dry him instead. If you decide to blow-dry him, use your pin brush as you're drying to keep the coat tangle-free.

HELP! MY CAVALIER'S COAT DOESN'T LOOK LIKE THOSE IN THE SHOW RING!

Many pet owners would like to get their pet to look more like those they see in the show ring. This section will help you achieve that.

When Cavaliers are neutered, the growth cycle of their coat lengthens, resulting in longer, sometimes wavier, and usually a more profuse coat. Also, older dogs tend to put on weight, and when they do, their coats tend to become even more profuse. One of the best ways to keep the coat growth down is to maintain your pet at a proper weight. This not only will be healthier for him but will also prevent an exceptionally profuse coat in most cases. However, even those in perfect weight will tend to get a fuzzier and longer coat after being neutered. Not all, but most.

After a full grooming session, take a stripping comb and comb in the direction of the coat. This will strip out all kinds of excess coat. You will need to stop often during a "stripping" session to remove your Cavalier's hair from the teeth of this tool. Keep going until he has a much sleeker-looking coat, but don't go too far the first time or two. It's best to do a little at a time until you find the right amount to strip.

After bathing your Cavalier and drying him as much as you can with a towel, put him on your chosen grooming surface and comb his hair straight. Then use a straightener product; you only need to use a tiny bit. Put a couple of drops on your hands, spread it around your hands, and carefully apply down the back of the coat and slightly down the sides. I usually do this three times, sometimes four. The first time is for the neck and shoulder area and down the sides, the second time is for the major back area and down the sides, and the final one is for the hindquarter area. Sometimes the hindquarters need to be done twice, concentrating on one side more the first time and then the other side.

Next carefully blow-dry your dog until he is nearly dry. Keep using the pin brush or a comb the whole time, always combing in the direction the coat lies. When your dog is dry to the touch with maybe a tiny amount of dampness in the undercoat, put a drying coat on him. A drying coat is a highly breathable but tightly fitting doggy coat that will help keep the coat from fluffing up while drying. Leave the drying coat on for a few hours until your dog is completely and totally dry. Then remove the coat and lightly brush your Cavalier out. You may also use a drying coat on a wet Cavalier, but this will take a lot longer because you will need to leave it on until he is completely dry.

Cut your Cavalier's nails regularly.

When done you will be amazed at how good your Cavalier looks—almost like those in the show ring!

NAIL CARE

Now it is time to check the nails and cut them if necessary. Many dogs who are well structured and spend some time each day walking on concrete, pavement, or gravel never need their nails cut. Others who spend their lives on

Dog Tale

If you decide to take your Cavalier to a professional groomer, please remember to tell her that your dog is a Cavalier and that he is supposed to look natural. I knew an owner who got her pet back the first time and he was thoroughly groomed like a Cocker Spaniel, with his entire back and ears shaved! It took months for his beautiful coat to grow back. Cavaliers are such natural and pretty little dogs; we don't want them looking like some other breed.

grass or carpeting will grow longer and longer nails unless the nails are regularly cut. They can grow so long that they will begin to splay the toes out, and eventually the nails will start to curl under, leading to an improper gait and eventually pain. Some nails may get so long that they curl around and begin to grow into the pads of the foot! To prevent this from happening, check the nails regularly and cut them if necessary.

HOW TO DO IT

Take your nail clipper of choice and pull the hair back from the nails. Then cut the nails just beyond where you can see the pink quick. Be careful because if you cut into the quick it will hurt and bleed. The quick is easy to see on most Blenheims because their nails tend to be white/opaque and you can see the pink quick right through it. The tricolors are not so hard either, but some do have some dark nails where you can't see through to the quick. Rubies and black-and-tans are the most difficult; most have dark nails and the quick cannot be seen. If this is the case with your Cavalier, look on the underside of his dark nails. You will usually be able to see an open part at the back of the end of the nail, and inside this opening the quick will be visible. Again, cut just beyond where the quick ends.

If you are cutting with a nail trimmer, you can also use a file, just as humans do, and file all the rough edges down afterward. The nails will be easier on your floors, your furniture, and especially your legs if you let your dog jump up to greet you. If you use a grinder you will need something to keep the hair out of the way, or you can keep the hair on the paws short. Then grind the nail down to just beyond the quick.

While cutting the nails, check the hair between the pads and cut it if it is longer than 1/2 inch (1.5 cm). This is very important to prevent matting and a big ball of hair from developing. Dogs who walk often on hard pavement will not get much hair growth between the pads, but those who live on grass and carpet almost certainly will.

For pets it is perfectly fine to cut the long feathering off the feet. This can make the nails easier to cut and help minimize bringing in huge snowballs, leaves, grass, and other "presents."

EAR CARE

Long-eared dogs tend to be prone to ear infections. It is hard to say whether your dog will be one of them, but you can sometimes predict the possibility. If your dog has higher-set ears, smaller and/or thinner ear leather, and does not have profuse ear feathering, he has a much better chance of not getting infections. Those dogs with lower-set ears, heavier/thicker ear leathers, and profuse ear feathering can be more prone because it is so much harder for air to flow inside.

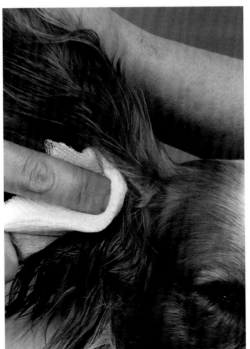

Clean your Cavalier's ears only if you see any real amount of dirt or wax.

HOW TO DO IT

Check the ears every time you groom your dog and clean them only if you see any real amount of dirt or wax. Try to clean the edges with a dry cotton ball, and use a cotton ball or gauze toward the canal.

If you do need to clean with a liquid solution, dry the ears very, very thoroughly afterward to prevent problems from starting. Many problems actually start due to constant cleaning with liquid and some moisture remaining behind, setting up the perfect conditions for the growth of yeast and bacteria. This is because the hanging flap of the ear prevents the free flow of air to the ear canal. If your dog has buildup often, it might help to trim a lot of hair out from under the ear flap, letting more air into the area. If the ears appear overly pink, have a foul smell, or there is a lot of buildup, it is time to contact your vet because your Cavalier may have an ear infection that needs to be treated.

EYE CARE

Check the eyes next. Some Cavaliers have prominent eyes, which can be more easily affected by wind and more prone to getting scratched. Some are prone to tearing as well.

HOW TO DO IT

When you groom your dog you can clean around the eyes with any good eye-cleaning solution; there are many on the market. You may use a soft cloth or tissue for this job. I prefer not to use cotton balls near the eyes because cotton fibers can shed and end up on the eyes, irritating them.

Note that many Cavalier puppies begin tearing when they start teething—at about four months of age. They may continue to have mild to profuse tearing through 10 to 12 months of age, after which time it starts to slow down considerably. I suggest that you refrain from trying to keep the area totally clean during this period. It seems to be that teething causes mild inflammation that puts pressure on the tear ducts, causing some blockage to natural drainage. Instead of tears pooling properly in the corners of the eyes and draining properly through the tear ducts, the tears spill out onto the face. The more you clean the more pressure you will put on the area, causing more inflammation and more tearing. If the tears really bother you, clean as lightly as you can about once a week to avoid putting pressure on the delicate eye tissues. If there is a buildup of hardened eye mucus, use a flea comb to gently clean this off, then finish gently cleaning the area with a soft cloth. Often the more you try to do, the worse the problem becomes.

PUPPY POINTER

Cavalier puppies often begin to show some eye tearing about the same time they begin teething. Once they reach about ten months of age this tearing will usually begin to go away, and by two years of age most or all of it will have stopped.

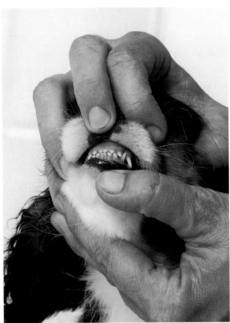

DENTAL CARE

Because our dogs today live and eat as we do, their teeth need the same kind of care that we need and for the same reasons. Plaque continually forms, and if not regularly removed, leads to tartar buildup. The bacteria in plaque may lead to gingivitis—an inflammation of the gums—or may get into the bloodstream, causing damage to the liver, kidneys, or heart valves. Left unchecked, tartar may lead to periodontal disease; the gums will recede, exposing the roots of the teeth, and eventually the teeth will become loose and fall out. For dogs with mitral valve disease (MVD), it is even more important to keep the teeth clean because bacteria and infection could get into the bloodstream and negatively affect the heart valves.

It is especially important to keep the teeth clean in dogs with mitral valve disease because an infection could get into the bloodstream and harm the heart.

Many toy breeds start needing to have teeth removed as young as seven years of age because they have small mouths with the teeth crowded closely together. It is not at all unusual to have a 12- or 13-year-old with few or no teeth at all. This rarely slows them down, though—they seem to eat just fine without teeth.

If you have a puppy, start brushing his teeth right away so that he gets used to it. You can use gauze or a finger toothbrush at first, graduating to a doggy toothbrush or a child's-size human toothbrush. Use doggy toothpaste; the menthol in human toothpaste will irritate his stomach.

HOW TO DO IT

While your Cavalier is still a puppy, you should start to clean his teeth from time to time. Use a doggy toothpaste, and for the first try it might be a good idea to put a bit of toothpaste right on your finger and offer him a smell and taste of it. Then begin to rub your finger over his teeth, letting him get used to how it feels. It is acceptable to use your finger or a cloth for the first few months, but eventually he will need to graduate to a real toothbrush. Once he has done so, you will need to clean his teeth in a more correct manner. Brush in a circular motion and tilt the toothbrush slightly downward for the top teeth and slightly upward for the bottom teeth to clean under the gums a bit better. Begin at the back of the mouth and work toward the front. The entire procedure should take about 30 seconds per section for a total of 2 minutes per full brushing. Always pay a bit more attention to the teeth in the back because they are the ones that tend to get the dirtiest. By the time your puppy is a year old, you should be brushing his teeth nearly every day. The older your Cavalier gets, the more often you will need to brush.

If plaque has really accumulated and/or the gums appear a bit redder at the gum line, it is time for a more thorough teeth cleaning. There are groups that do anesthesia-free cleaning for a price. This can be a wonderful alternative if the teeth are not overly dirty or if your pet is older and on heart medication. Vets can also perform teeth cleanings, but they nearly always use a general anesthesia. Try to limit an anesthetic cleaning to once a year if possible.

SENIOR CARE
Older dogs should be groomed more often because they are increasingly prone to getting lumps and bumps, especially sebaceous cysts. Inspect these regularly

Older dogs should be groomed more often because they are increasingly prone to getting lumps and bumps, and a grooming session may help you spot them.

A professional groomer can help your Cavalier look his best.

in case they start to grow to a size that is more prone to rubbing and injury; they may also turn out to be something more serious, such as cancer.

The teeth need to be inspected more often too because they get dirtier more quickly, and some may need to be removed. As mentioned previously, this is important to prevent infection from getting into the bloodstream and affecting the heart. Unfortunately, most Cavaliers past 13 or 14 years of age will eventually get to the point where it is dangerous to be put under general anesthesia for a thorough teeth cleaning.

Some really old dogs become unstable and may need to be groomed on their sides on a bed—one side at a time. Even at this age, groom regularly and keep it enjoyable. Make this a special time for your aging Cavalier.

FINDING A PROFESSIONAL GROOMER

Some people find it easier to take their Cavalier to a groomer than to groom him themselves. You can find groomers in the telephone book and online, or talk to your vet, friends, or neighbors to get a recommendation. Show people tend to know the best groomers. Some larger pet-supply stores often have groomers who work for them.

Look for a groomer who has a warm way with animals and who doesn't need to use a sedative to calm your dog. If your dog looks great after being groomed and looks forward to going to that groomer the next time, you know that you have a good one. If your dog acts anxious or scared or doesn't look good after being groomed, it is probably time to find someone new.

CHAPTER 6

HEALTH OF YOUR CAVALIER KING CHARLES SPANIEL

Your Cavalier puppy is a live animal. You cannot expect perfection, no matter how well he was bred. Cavaliers are just like humans—none of us is perfect. Testing, in general, reduces the number of different health problems in a breed and also reduces the severity of those problems, but it does not eliminate them except in the case of single-gene traits. Unfortunately, most health problems involve more than one gene.

Environment also plays a large part in whether or not your Cavalier will lead a decently healthy long life. Good veterinary care helps, but you can also do things to encourage better health. As a rule, good food, regular exercise, and especially keeping your Cavalier at a proper weight will be the most important things you can do. In a breed in which your Cavalier will almost certainly develop mitral valve disease (MVD) at some point, an overweight Cavalier is nearly guaranteed to succumb. Being overweight is quite likely to cause him to develop MVD earlier than his genetics dictated and will definitely put extra stress on the heart, causing premature death.

THE VETERINARIAN

If you don't already have a vet, talk to friends and family about vets whom they know or have heard of. Call your local breed club; breeders in your area will know the very best vets for their breed. Visit a few vets before you get your puppy—most vets are happy to talk to prospective clients.

It is best if your vet knows something about the Cavalier breed. And never discount a younger vet! Most young vets are still enthusiastic about doing the best job and also have better ears for hearing murmurs. Don't use a vet who makes you or your puppy uncomfortable or who won't listen to you.

Schedule your puppy's first appointment for a few days after you bring him home.

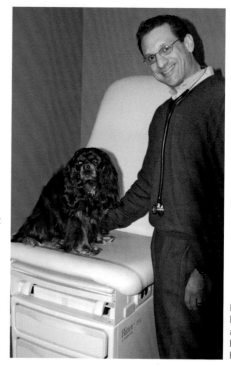

It's best if your vet knows something about the Cavalier breed and its specific health issues.

FIRST VISIT TO THE VET

At his first appointment, your Cavalier won't need shots or a fecal check because the breeder will have already had that done. This visit is mostly to reassure you and your vet that your puppy is as healthy as stated. Your vet should give him a thorough checkup and ask you lots of questions regarding his activity level and eating and eliminating habits, as well as asking you whether you have any other questions or concerns.

If your breeder has not already done so, your vet can show you how to trim nails and give you other tips. This visit should be a pleasant one for your puppy. Schedule the following visit for when the next vaccination booster is due.

ANNUAL VET VISIT

Your Cavalier should see his vet about once a year after all his puppy shots have been given. Once he has reached about ten years of age (earlier if he has begun to have MVD symptoms), he should visit the vet twice a year. During his last year of life the visits may have to be increased even more. We all die of something, and most of us will need increased medical care the last year or so of our lives.

Your vet should do the following at each annual checkup:
- check the feces for internal parasites
- look for external parasites and lumps and bumps or dandruff
- listen carefully to the heart to see whether a murmur has developed or to follow the progression of a murmur if he previously developed one
- listen to his lungs to make sure that they are clear
- check the anal sacs
- thoroughly inspect the abdomen
- check the teeth and gums and look inside the mouth to see whether there are any other problems
- manipulate the knees to see whether patellar luxation is present or getting worse
- check the eyes for excess discharge and cataracts
- check the ears to be sure that they are clean and odor-free
- watch him walk around on the floor to see whether there are any skeletal issues or the beginnings of arthritis or any nervous system abnormalities
- talk with you extensively to see whether there have been any changes in his behavior or in his eating and eliminating habits

SPAYING AND NEUTERING

Spaying and neutering are the names given to the processes of removing all or most of a dog's reproductive organs so that he or she can no longer reproduce. The word "neuter" can be used for both sexes, but the word "spay" is used only for females.

There has been much controversy in the last several years over when it's the right time to spay or neuter pets. Most of the health benefits of neutering young are the same as neutering a bit later, when the growth plates are closed. For instance, testicular cancer and prostate problems are nearly eliminated in males once neutered, whether it be at 2 to 6 months or 12 to 15 months. The same is true in the female, but there is one definite health benefit in that the chance for the development of mammary tumors is reduced in females who are spayed before they ever go into season. The biggest benefits to neutering overall are that roaming is reduced and the chance of pregnancy eliminated.

There are, however, many disadvantages with regard to overall health and negative effects to skeletal health when neutering young. Lots of research has been conducted on this subject. Refer to the Bibliography for websites to visit to read more about this.

Generally it is almost certainly better to wait to spay or neuter until after your Cavalier's growth plates have closed. In females this occurs at 10 to 12 months of age and in males by 12 to 15 months of age. But most of all, be a responsible owner! If there is any chance at all that your dog might get out and become pregnant or get another dog pregnant, please spay or neuter early.

VACCINATIONS

A vaccination is the introduction of a substance into the body to cause the body to produce antibodies and create immunity to a disease. Vaccinations can be divided into core and noncore vaccines, and there is a specified schedule for their administration.

The most common reactions include acting a bit depressed or "down" for a few days. Some dogs may exhibit swelling in the vaccination site area or breathing difficulties. Truly serious reactions are quite rare.

CORE VACCINES

Core vaccines are considered most important and include those given to prevent distemper, hepatitis, parvovirus, and rabies. There is no real treatment for these diseases save relief of symptoms until the disease has run its course. For instance, if the dog is dehydrated, the veterinarian will give IV fluids and so on. Occasionally an antibiotic may be given to support the dog's immune system because it may be severely compromised by the disease. For this reason, it is best to have your dog vaccinated against these diseases.

Distemper

Canine distemper is a viral disease that despite extensive vaccination remains a major disease in some regions. Symptoms consist of fever, respiratory problems, and gastrointestinal issues that progress to other, more severe symptoms. Puppies from three to six months old are particularly susceptible and experience the highest mortality rate because of complications.

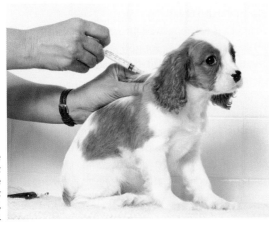

Core vaccines are considered most important and include those given to prevent distemper, hepatitis, parvovirus, and rabies.

Hepatitis

Infectious canine hepatitis is an acute liver infection in dogs caused by canine adenovirus type-1 (CAV-1). Symptoms include fever, depression, loss of appetite, coughing, and a tender abdomen. Death can occur secondary to liver disease, but most dogs recover after a brief illness without treatment.

Parvovirus

Parvovirus is a highly contagious virus affecting dogs. The disease is spread from dog to dog by direct or indirect contact with their feces. It can be especially severe in puppies who are not protected by maternal antibodies or vaccination. Vaccines can prevent this infection, but mortality can be extremely high in untreated cases.

Rabies

Rabies is a viral disease that is usually fatal. The vaccine is also the only vaccine required by US state law. Rabies is transmitted through the bite of an infected mammal such as a cat, raccoon, or another dog. Animals with rabies suffer deterioration of the brain and tend to behave bizarrely and often aggressively, increasing the chances that they will bite another animal or a person and transmit the disease. Death is usually caused by respiratory arrest.

NONCORE VACCINES

Noncore vaccines are considered optional and include those against bordetella, coronavirus, leptospirosis, Lyme disease, and parainfluenza.

Bordetella

Bordetella is a bacterium that causes cold symptoms similar to those produced by the whooping cough in humans and is part of the kennel cough family. Symptoms can vary from the mildest possible upper respiratory infection to a very serious one—just as with the human cold. Mild cases usually need no treatment at all, but severe ones may need to be treated with antibiotics and bronchodilators that relax the air passages in the lungs and make breathing easier.

Note that the vaccine for bordetella is not long lived (protection is usually for considerably less than one year) so should not be routinely administered annually. It is best to have your pet vaccinated only when needed instead—about a month before you will be boarding your dog in a kennel.

Coronavirus

Coronavirus primarily infects the upper respiratory and gastrointestinal tract of mammals and birds. It tends to produce very mild symptoms, like diarrhea, vomiting, and some lack of interest in eating, in all but the most immunocompromised dogs. Again, treatment consists only of support: administration of IV fluids if the dog is dehydrated or medication to reduce diarrhea.

Leptospirosis

Leptospira is a bacterium that is very common in parts of the United States. Dogs most commonly infected are those who are outdoors with exposure to surface water, as the most common route of disease transmission is indirect, by contact with stagnant or slow-moving water contaminated by urine from infected animals. The most common signs of disease early on are anorexia, lethargy, vomiting, and fever. Fortunately, the disease is rarely fatal. Treatment consists of antibiotic therapy to reduce the duration of the disease, to reduce the time the dog is contagious, and to reduce damage to the kidneys and liver. Supportive treatment may also be necessary. The leptospirosis vaccine is known to be one of those that cause the highest percentage of negative reactions.

Lyme Disease

Lyme disease is caused by infected ticks that attach to a dog for several days while feeding. The disease causes symptoms such as joint inflammation (polyarthritis), which is first seen as lameness. Most dogs who test positive do not show symptoms. If the dog shows symptoms, a prescription medication is used for one month, with most dogs showing improvement in just one to two days. The vaccination for Lyme should be avoided. It has already been withdrawn from use for humans, as the side effects are usually worse than the disease and treatment works well.

Dogs who spend a lot of time outdoors in grassy or heavily wooded areas may be more prone to contracting Lyme disease.

Parainfluenza

Parainfluenza is similar to bordetella in that it is a kennel cough-type infection that causes mild respiratory symptoms. Treatment is the same as for bordetella.

VACCINATION SCHEDULE

Depending on where you live and what type of lifestyle your Cavalier leads, his vaccination schedule may vary. The following is a good commonsense schedule that will work for most healthy Cavaliers.

- 8, 12, and 16 weeks: distemper and

parvo puppy shots
- 6 months: first rabies booster
- 16 months: combo vaccine; every 3 years thereafter: combo vaccine
- 18 months: second rabies booster
- rabies vaccine per state law
- bordetella as needed, not annually

PARASITES

A parasite is a living organism that feeds, grows, and lives on (external parasites) or inside (internal parasites) a separate life form only for its own survival. It contributes nothing to the survival of—and in fact can be very harmful to—the life form.

FLEAS AND TICKS

Fleas are pretty easy to spot; it's getting rid of them that may be hard. The first sign usually is that your dog scratches himself a lot. His skin may have small red spots, and his coat may have small black spots left from the fleas.

Ticks are a little different. They can bite your dog and latch on while in heavily wooded or grassy areas. If he has been bitten by a tick, quick action is required to remove the tick to reduce the risk of Lyme disease. You can remove a tick by

Check your Cavalier for fleas and ticks after he's been playing outside.

using tweezers. Grasp as much of the tick as you can with the tweezers and pull straight out with a steady motion. Keep an eye on the area for several days just in case an infection sets in.

Both fleas and ticks are easily controlled by topical or internal medications your vet can supply.

PUPPY POINTER

Buy a responsibly bred puppy if you want to minimize health problems (and expenses).

HEARTWORMS

Heartworm is spread by mosquitoes. It starts out as tiny larvae called microfilariae. The larvae can be detected by a simple heartworm test in which the vet draws blood and looks for the larvae under a microscope. If left untreated, the larvae will move to the dog's heart, where they continue to grow until they completely clog up the heart and eventually cause death. To prevent heartworm, a monthly preventive may be given. If you live in an area where it freezes over in the winter, you may opt to not give a heartworm preventive year round.

HOOKWORMS

Hookworms derive their name from their hook-like mouth parts consisting of teeth-like structures or cutting plates with which they attach themselves to the intestinal wall. These parasites feed on the blood of the host animal. Hookworm infection can lead to severe anemia and diarrhea. This infection can sometimes be lethal to puppies if not attended to properly. The most common symptoms of hookworm infection include pale-colored gums and stunted growth in young animals.

ROUNDWORMS

Roundworms are the most common intestinal parasites found in puppies, which are often infected at birth or soon thereafter. Roundworms in dogs can result in a potbelly, poor coat, slow growth, vomiting, and diarrhea. Severe cases may even lead to intestinal blockage, rupture, or even death.

WHIPWORMS

Whipworms are parasites that live in a dog's large intestine. The whipworm gets its name from the adult worm's characteristic whip-like shape, with the front end narrower than the back end. Infection of a dog occurs only when he accidentally ingests whipworm eggs containing infective larvae or juvenile worms. Whipworms can cause diarrhea, weight loss, and anemia.

BREED-SPECIFIC HEALTH ISSUES

Like all other breeds, Cavaliers have health issues. Responsible breeders should be testing their breeding stock to make educated breeding choices. Health screening clinics across the country are becoming ever more popular. The Orthopedic Foundation for Animals (OFA) (www.offa.org) began listing test results for hip dysplasia many years ago. Over the years the OFA has expanded to include the results of many other inherited problems such as elbow dysplasia, patellar luxation, inherited eye problems, heart problems, thyroid disorders, and more. Today they include vertical pedigree analysis where you can see the results of parents and family members all together. The American Kennel Club (AKC) (www.akc.org) joined in and began the Canine Health Information Center (CHIC) (www.caninehealthinfo.org). Breed clubs choose which tests are necessary, and dogs who have been tested for all of them are awarded a CHIC number. Each of these sites can help you in choosing a puppy from a responsibly bred litter.

This section describes some of the most common problems in Cavaliers.

EPILEPSY

Epilepsy is a neurological condition that causes seizures. True epilepsy is not all that common in this breed. Most seizures may well be attributed to hydrocephalus (water on the brain) and/or syringomyelia (SM). (See section below.) Just as in humans and in all other dog breeds, it does seem to occur occasionally. If the seizures happen often and regularly, your dog can be treated with a drug that may reduce or eliminate seizure activity.

EPISODIC FALLING SYNDROME (EFS)

A dog with this syndrome will suddenly become rigid/freeze and/or collapse, can't move for a period of time, and then recover. Episodes can last from seconds to minutes, and dogs recover completely each time. Most Cavaliers who develop this disorder will do so by five months of age, although it can appear at any age. The dog will not lose consciousness during episodes, making it different from a seizure disorder. Episodic falling syndrome is seldom life threatening. Extended episodes can be shortened by treatment with a drug. EFS is caused by a simple recessive gene, and there is now a genetic test available to test for it.

A dog with episodic falling syndrome will suddenly become unable to move for a time but then recover.

FLY CATCHER'S SYNDROME

A Cavalier who has fly catcher's syndrome has seizure-like episodes in which he looks as if he is trying to catch a fly. This disease may be related to epilepsy and usually responds well to the same drugs.

HIP DYSPLASIA

Hip dysplasia occurs when the hip socket in one or both hips does not form correctly. Although Cavaliers are a small breed, this disease is fairly common—probably between 15 and 25 percent are affected. If your Cavalier seems to show pain in his hindquarters when first standing up or after playing awhile, he may have hip dysplasia. A simple X-ray will diagnose the problem.

For milder cases, keeping your Cavalier thin and on a joint supplement will be enough, as might control of pain with medication. Cavaliers rarely need surgery, but it has happened. They are too small for hip replacement surgery; instead the surgery of choice is to cut off the ball of the hip joint, called the femoral head. This seems to alleviate pain in most Cavaliers.

KERATOCONJUNCTIVITIS SICCA (KCS)

KCS, also called dry eye, occurs when there is inadequate tear production. In response the eye will create a sticky substance in an effort to protect the eye. If you constantly see a thick, gooey substance in your dog's eyes and he is constantly blinking or the surface of his eyes appears dry and dull (possibly leading to chronic ulcers), there is a simple test that can be done to diagnose dry eye. Treatment consists of special eyedrops that will need to be put in your dog's eyes daily, possibly for the rest of his life. Although rare, some dogs do recover from dry eye.

Many Cavaliers have more prominent eyes than most other breeds, and they can be prone to injury and ulceration. Make sure that you carefully check your Cavalier's eyes at every grooming session.

MITRAL VALVE DISEASE (MVD)

MVD is a developmental disease of the heart in which the mitral valve ages more rapidly than it should. The mitral valve is supposed to open to let blood flow through but close immediately so that blood doesn't flow backward. With MVD the collagen in the valve breaks down prematurely and the valve becomes progressively sloppier, not closing as well as it used to and letting some blood flow backward. Over time the valve gets ever sloppier, closes even more poorly, and even more blood flows backward, making the heart work ever harder to get oxygen to the tissues. The heart increases in size to compensate.

MVD is the most common health concern of Cavaliers today. You can assume that your Cavalier will develop MVD at some point. Don't listen to breeders who say that only 50 percent develop it or that there is no MVD in their lines, as these are not true statements. Yes, there are some Cavaliers who never develop MVD, but this is quite rare. Your concern should be the general ages the parents and grandparents were when they developed MVD. Were they young, aged three to four; average, aged five to seven; or older, aged eight years and up, when they first developed MVD? Chances are your Cavalier will follow in their footsteps to some extent.

Sufficient exercise will help keep your Cavalier healthy.

BE AWARE!

The following is a list of common medical emergencies and what you can do to help. However, as soon as you've stabilized the situation, take your dog to the vet.

Convulsion/Seizure
Signs: *Drooling, stiffness, muscle spasms, involuntary urination or defecation.*
Treatment: *Wrap dog in blanket and keep him from injuring himself; keep away from his mouth until seizure is over.*

Heatstroke
Signs: *Rapid loud breathing, abundant thick saliva, bright red mucous membranes, and high temperature progressing to unsteady walk, diarrhea, and coma.*
Treatment: *Wet him down starting with cool water (not ice cold!) at first. Offer him water. Keep taking his temperature, making sure that his body temperature is slowly coming down. It may take a few days for him to recover.*

Hypoglycemia
Signs: *Appears disoriented, weak, staggers, may appear blind, muscles may twitch; can progress to convulsions, coma, and death.*
Treatment: *Give food, honey, or syrup mixed with warm water and monitor his condition.*

Hypothermia
Signs: *Shivering, cold body, sluggishness.*
Treatment: *Slowly warm him up in a blanket, checking his temperature often to see that his body temperature is slowly rising to normal.*

Open Wound
Signs: *Open bleeding wound. A wound is an emergency if there is profuse bleeding, if it is extremely deep, or if the wound is open all the way into the chest cavity (where the heart and lungs are), the abdominal cavity (where the intestines are), or the skull into the brain.*
Treatment: *Control massive bleeding first. Cover wound with clean dressing and apply pressure. Elevate wound site, apply cold pack. Pressure should be applied on side of wound toward the heart. If a head wound, monitor for consciousness and shock. If an abdominal wound, cover organs with sterile dressing and cover with towel.*

Shock
Signs: *Weakness, collapse, pale gums, unresponsiveness, faint pulse.*
Treatment: *Can occur in almost any case of trauma, so treat for shock even if not sure he is experiencing it. Keep him warm and quiet, and keep the head low compared to his heart (unless he has a head wound).*

After mitral valve disease has progressed sufficiently, your Cavalier will begin to develop symptoms such as difficulty catching his breath and tiring easily.

A murmur is the first symptom of MVD and can be heard with a stethoscope. Murmurs go from a grade 1, the softest murmur, to a grade 6, which you can hear without a stethoscope. Cardiologists are much better at hearing grade 1 murmurs than most regular vets, which is why breeders should have their breeding stock checked once a year by a board-certified cardiologist rather than a vet. You might even want to check with area breed clubs for health screening clinics in your area. At a clinic, a cardiologist can check your Cavalier once a year for considerably less money than it would cost to visit one privately. This information on your dog will not only help you, but it will also help your breeder do a better job.

When a murmur first develops your Cavalier will not have other symptoms and will not need treatment. It is only after the MVD has progressed sufficiently that your Cavalier will begin to develop symptoms such as difficulty catching his breath, tiring easily, and coughing. (It may be a good idea to get a base chest X-ray right at the beginning so that subsequent X-rays can be compared to the original to see the progression of heart enlargement.) Cavaliers vary greatly in how long they stay in this phase—some will progress in just a few months while others may continue to have a grade 1 murmur for as long as ten years! In most cases, the better the heart history, the slower your Cavalier's MVD will progress—even if developed earlier than his ancestors developed MVD.

Once your Cavalier develops symptoms, he will need to start medication. As MVD progresses, other medications may need to be added. Cavaliers can do quite well with MVD for many years if controlled correctly. Your vet will be able to handle most of the care, but you might want to throw in an occasional cardiologist visit for even better management of the disease. A chest X-ray should be done from time to time to see how the heart is doing and how enlarged it is becoming. Despite all of this, many Cavaliers will actually die from something else.

Note that many Cavalier puppies have innocent "flow" murmurs at their first few checkups. These murmurs are not related to MVD. Most of them disappear by six months of age and rarely continue for a year or more.

PATELLAR LUXATION

The patella is the kneecap. Dogs have a kneecap on each hind leg, just as humans do. The patella normally sits in a groove, held tightly by ligaments. However, many Cavaliers develop luxating patellas, a condition in which the kneecap becomes loose and pops out of the groove often—and sometimes permanently stays outside the groove. This is amazingly common in poorly bred Cavaliers, with as many as three-quarters of them affected, whereas only a very small percentage of responsibly bred Cavaliers whose parents were tested clear are affected. Symptoms are hind-leg lameness, a hopping gait, and occasionally carrying the affected leg up. Some Cavaliers may learn to throw their hind leg out to put the patella back in place.

Very mild cases can be controlled by keeping your Cavalier thin and using a joint supplement. More severe cases require surgery. This surgery is costly, and it's not always successful. You would be smarter to buy a dog only from a responsible breeder who tests for patellar luxation, as you will greatly decrease the possibility that your Cavalier will be affected. Also note the high likelihood that a poorly bred Cavalier will need surgery, negating any savings in purchasing a less expensive Cavalier from an irresponsible breeder.

PRIMARY SECRETORY OTITIS MEDIA (PSOM)

PSOM is a condition in Cavaliers that is similar to glue ear in children, a condition in which thick, sticky fluid collects behind the eardrum. In severe cases it can cause deafness. Some symptoms of PSOM include ear scratching and head shaking and may also possibly include neurological effects, although these may be hard to separate from SM effects. PSOM can be diagnosed by an MRI (magnetic resonance imaging). The treatment of choice is surgery, but recurrence is common.

REVERSE SNEEZING

A dog who is reverse sneezing stands and acts as though he can't get enough air. Although it looks frightening, this condition is not dangerous. It is caused by the spasming of an elongated soft palate. You can stop an episode quickly by gently bending the head down toward the chest to make a curve in the neck—this seems to stretch the palate out and stops the spasms almost instantly. In typical cases no treatment is necessary or even available. If the episodes happen frequently (many times a day), there may be other causes that should be investigated by a veterinarian.

SYRINGOMYELIA (SM)

SM is a common neurological disorder in Cavaliers caused by a backskull that is not large enough to accommodate the cerebellum—a part of the brain. Because there is not enough room, the cerebellum is squashed up against the foramen magnum, the opening at the back of the skull where the spinal cord goes through. This causes a vacuum and pressure changes, and eventually small pockets of fluid form inside the spinal cord, which leads to various neurological problems. Almost unheard of 25 years ago, SM has skyrocketed to become the second-most prevalent problem in Cavaliers. What is most amazing is that most Cavaliers with SM don't appear to have any symptoms, or symptoms are so mild as not to be noticed.

The most common symptom of SM is pain, especially headache. You may notice that your Cavalier seems to not want to move his head around much or may have a pained or strained look in his eyes. Some Cavaliers with SM may yawn

If your Cavalier has syringomyelia, you may notice that he doesn't want to move his head much or may have a pained look in his eyes.

more often than normal to relieve pressure. About 30 percent of those affected may scratch at their neck excessively, especially when excited or on leash, leading owners and veterinarians to believe at first that the dog has allergies. Some will experience seizures because of SM. In more severe cases, symptoms may include leg lameness (signal to move the leg is not getting to the leg or signal is getting "scrambled"); an inability to feel the floor (looks as though dog is walking on eggshells or doesn't quite know where the floor is); a twisted spine; and occasional screaming and writhing in agony for minutes at a time. It is especially heartbreaking to witness these severely painful episodes.

The only way to diagnose SM conclusively is by MRI. This is a very expensive test. Most SM symptoms can be controlled by medications such as gabapentin (neurontin) or diuretics, which help reduce the amount of fluid and can reduce some pressure. If symptoms are severe or progressing rapidly, surgery is another viable albeit expensive option. Although relapses may occur, most dogs will recover and do quite well after surgery.

Research is still ongoing, but at the very least breeders should be starting to MRI their breeding stock and breeding for more backskull in their dogs.

THROMBOCYTOPENIA

Approximately 30 percent of all Cavaliers have very large but less numerous blood platelets. These should be hand-counted because machines often miss them. The larger platelets seem to do just as good a job as the more numerous smaller ones.

Don't worry if your vet finds that your Cavalier has a very low platelet count. If he doesn't show other signs, such as excessive bleeding, he is probably just fine. The typical Cavalier with thrombocytopenia has no symptoms and no treatment is needed.

UMBILICAL HERNIAS

An umbilical hernia occurs when the hole in the abdominal cavity where the umbilicus was attached (belly button) does not close entirely at or shortly after birth, occasionally letting parts of the intestines partially protrude through the hole. This condition is quite common in Cavaliers.

The vast majority of umbilical hernias close up by six months or so, leaving nothing but a bit of tissue on the outside, which creates that small bump you see. This is not truly a hernia because there is no longer an actual opening in the abdominal cavity wall. You may opt to leave it as is or have it surgically corrected during another surgery, such as a spay or neuter. In essence you are not having anything repaired; this is more along the lines of plastic surgery in that you are just making it look "prettier." In rare instances, the opening may not close and surgery to close it will need to be performed.

GENERAL ILLNESS

General illness occurs when there is a breakdown in the function of the immune or other system, which causes poor health in the body or mind. The following paragraphs will address a few of the more common types of illnesses in dogs.

ALLERGIES

Dogs can develop allergies to just about anything. Symptoms can range from itching to hives to vomiting to diarrhea—and sometimes chronic ear infections can be the result of an allergy. You may have to look at your dog's environment to see what is causing his allergic reaction. For instance, the cleaning agents used when cleaning carpeting are a common culprit, and some dogs develop seasonal allergies to pollen. Sometimes all that is needed is a diet change or elimination of a particular food or the offending agent. If symptoms are serious, a visit to the vet is needed. Dogs can get allergy shots to desensitize them to the allergen.

Special note: if your Cavalier's itching seems to always be in one specific place or on one side only or if symptoms seem to escalate when he is excited or during weather changes, he may instead be exhibiting symptoms of syringomyelia. Many Cavaliers are treated for allergies when they actually have SM. (See section on SM for more information.)

CANCER

Cancer is as common in dogs as it is in humans. They can get any type of cancer that humans get. Lumps or bumps that suddenly change shape or start growing, changes in eating or eliminating habits, or sudden weight loss or gain can all be indications of cancer. If you're concerned, visit the vet for a thorough examination. Treatment can include surgery, chemotherapy, and/or radiation. Cure is possible if the cancer is caught early.

Dogs can develop allergies to just about anything, including pollen.

Ear infections are much more common in breeds that have hanging ears because there is less airflow to the ear canal.

EAR INFECTIONS

Ear infections are much more common in breeds that have hanging ears because there is less airflow to the ear canal. If your Cavalier's ears look inflamed or have excessive discharge or a foul odor, he probably has an ear infection. Some Cavaliers will paw at their ears or rub them on the carpeting to get relief. Your vet can treat the condition with a topical (external) antibiotic-based ear cleaner or an internal antibiotic if the infection is severe.

ALTERNATIVE THERAPIES

Many owners today are turning to alternative care because it is often a gentler course of action than conventional medicine—and it works! Alternative therapies can be used alone or in conjunction with standard Western drug treatment. They are often the best way to go with regard to allergies and pain relief.

ACUPUNCTURE

Acupuncture has been around for thousands of years. It treats the body as a sort of electrical energy field (which is what it is!) in which something has gone out of whack. Tiny needles are inserted at acupoints to help redirect the energy or electricity in an attempt to fix the problem. Acupuncture can be used for pain relief, to increase blood flow, to lower heart rate, and to improve immune function.

CHIROPRACTIC

Chiropractic treatment consists of realigning bones that may be out of position due to strenuous activities. This is popular with owners who participate in performance events with their Cavaliers and with owners of aging Cavaliers.

HERBAL

Some herbal remedies can be a gentler and safer alternative to traditional Western medicine but not always. Remember that most Western medications start out with a "natural" source too. Used incorrectly, herbal therapies may actually be less safe, and when combined with Western medicine, may seriously compromise the benefits that traditional medicine offers.

HOMEOPATHY

Homeopathy is based on the premise that "like cures like." A substance is used that normally causes the disease, but it is diluted in several stages so that it is safe and free from side effects. However, the body is able to recognize the substance and eventually heal itself.

THE SENIOR CAVALIER

Nearly all of my Cavaliers have lived to 13 to 15 years of age and a few beyond that. Many of my 12- to 13-year-olds still act like puppies! But eventually, barring an accident, they all get old. Just like humans, they will need more attention and medical care as they age.

Your Cavalier will need more attention and medical care as he ages.

COMMON CHANGES

Many changes will need to be made as your dog ages.

- **Vet checks:** Vet checks should now take place twice a year and possibly more often during the final year of life.
- **Eating habits:** It is even more important to keep your Cavalier at a healthy weight with a good-

quality diet. Some dogs may have to be enticed to eat as age gets really advanced. Look for serious appetite changes because they may indicate cancer.

- **Bone and joint care:** Softer bedding should be provided to comfort arthritic or otherwise painful joints and bones. A good joint supplement such as glucosamine and/or chondroitin may need to be added.
- **Dental care:** The teeth should be checked more closely, although at some point cleaning may have to be stopped if your Cavalier's mitral valve disease has progressed to a point where general anesthesia is dangerous.
- **Hearing and sight loss:** Hearing and sight will also probably be starting to go. Most of my 15- to 16-year-olds have some sight and hearing loss, but they cope very well with it. Make sure that your Cavalier still gets exercise, though.
- **Senility:** He may act senile or as if he has Alzheimer's disease, so you may have to do more for him. Some vets may call this canine cognitive dysfunction (CCD). Your Cavalier may forget his housetraining, change his wake/sleep habits, wander around the house all night long, forget where things are, behave disorientedly, or seek less human attention. This is due to both physical and mental changes as he ages. There is a drug available that may help in some cases.
- **Incontinence:** Some Cavaliers will have some bladder control loss, especially those who have serious mitral valve disease and are on certain medications for it. You may have to come up with alternatives in that case.

SAYING GOODBYE

You may be lucky and your Cavalier may die peacefully in his sleep, but in most cases he will eventually get to the point where you realize that his quality of life is so low that it's time to say goodbye.

You may make his last day a special one. You can also ask to have the body back to bury, or you may opt to have him cremated. Most vets will put the ashes in a very nice urn-type box. A lot of vets offer a small plaque with the dog's name and paw print too. It will be a sad day, but take time to remember your beloved friend's good days. And when you are ready, you can always add another canine member to your family.

TRAINING YOUR
CAVALIER KING
CHARLES SPANIEL

Why should you train your Cavalier? He will be easier to live with and will be happier as well. Dogs are pack animals by nature—make sure that your dog is part of your pack!

I would estimate Cavalier trainability as medium to high. Despite what has been said about Cavaliers, they tend to be very intelligent and easy to train. Although there may be the occasional stubborn Cavalier, most have a high desire to please and will turn themselves inside out to please their owners.

TRAINING TIPS

Start training the moment you get your Cavalier puppy home. Remember, he is a dog, not a human child, so treat him like a dog. And don't expect him to be a statue—your puppy is a live animal with a brain, so he needs something to do!

The following are some basic training tips to help you get started.

ASSEMBLE YOUR SUPPLIES

One of the very best training aids available is a clicker. A clicker is a small plastic box with a metal "tongue" on it. When you push the tongue down, it makes a distinct clicking sound, marking a desired behavior the instant that your dog performs it. If you'd like a dog who will *want* to learn and will respond with excitement, clicker training is the way to go. However, if a clicker isn't for you, you can also use a marker word—like "yes!"—to mark a desired behavior in the same way that a clicker does.

Always have a collar and leash for training and for walks. A buckle or nylon collar is fine. Another good thing to have is a 20-foot (6-m) leash for outside *recall* training.

You may also use treats to encourage proper behavior. If you are going to do so, use tiny-sized treats that are easy to quickly chew and swallow. Their tiny size is also less likely to add too many calories to your dog's daily intake, helping him maintain his weight. You can buy training treats, but you may also use your dog's own kibble if the pieces

A buckle or nylon collar will work well for training your Cavalier.

are tiny, or make some treats of your own. Some dogs love veggie hot dogs or liver, which can be cut into tiny pieces and cooked or microwaved until they are fairly dry and crunchy.

EMPLOY POSITIVE TRAINING

Positive training is a method that uses lots of praise and rewards rather than correction or punishment to teach your dog correct behavior. You can train a dog using only praise and rewards, and in fact, unless your timing is excellent, it may be best to never correct. Rewards can be in the form of treats, praise, physical affection, toys, or whatever it is that your dog considers a reward.

Dogs' temperaments vary, but as long as your Cavalier is happy in responding to your commands, you will know that you are praising enough. If he isn't performing, there is something wrong—either you're not praising enough or he may just be confused. Evaluate what you are doing wrong and fix it. If you don't know, seek professional help. Your puppy will eventually learn what he can and cannot do and will grow to be a well-behaved dog.

UTILIZE GOOD TIMING

Cavaliers are dogs, and dogs are quite literal and very in the moment. Timing is critical; poor timing will only confuse your dog. For instance, if you correct your dog, he will always believe that you are correcting him for what he is thinking or doing at the exact moment you begin to do so—not for something he did 5 minutes ago or even 30 seconds ago!

CHOOSE THE RIGHT WORDS

When training your dog, use one-word phrases and choose simple words so as not to confuse him. Never use his name with stationary commands such as *sit* and *stay* because most dogs will want to come to you when they hear their name, not remain in a stationary command. And until you are certain that your dog will come to you every time you call him, it is better to use only his name without the word "come."

WORK ON YOUR BODY LANGUAGE

Never forget that you are always training your Cavalier. Dogs had to learn to read body language really well in the wild. If they didn't learn quickly, they didn't survive. This means that your dog is always watching you and learning from you, even when you are not actively training him and even when you are doing things that do not involve him at all.

Cavaliers are very easy to train as long as their owner treats them and trains them with positive encouragement and respect.

MAKE TRAINING A GAME

If you really want your puppy to respond immediately, make it a game! Don't just train him during a training session. If you are walking through a room and your puppy is following you, very suddenly say "Sit" or "Down" or whatever command you choose once. Then praise like crazy, releasing him from the commanded position immediately. Very quickly your puppy will learn to respond almost instantaneously, almost as if it is a game to outthink you. Formal training sessions are necessary and good, but these quickie lessons really put the zip into the response and will get him excited. In addition, they also reinforce that your dog must obey at all times, not just during a training session.

GO TO AN OBEDIENCE CLASS

I strongly advise that all Cavalier owners take their puppies to obedience class, more to train the owner than the dog. By the time he is three to four months of age you should get your puppy into a kindergarten class. Later, after about one year of age, attend a formal obedience class. Cavaliers are very easy to train as long as their owners treat them and train them with positive encouragement and respect. More on how to find an obedience class will be discussed toward the end of the chapter.

SOCIALIZATION

Socialization is a process that helps your puppy experience all kinds of situations so that he may adjust to the world and become a better behaved member of your family as a result. He needs to learn to accept strangers, unusual sights such as people in hats, noises such as the vacuum cleaner, and new situations such as a visit to the vet so that he will be happy and confident, not fearful and anxious. Dogs who are fearful and anxious are more likely to act out in aggressive ways or to develop problem behaviors such as chewing destructively or barking out of control.

Socialization should have been started while your dog was with his mom and breeder, but you need to continue it from the moment you bring him home.

HOW TO SOCIALIZE

Even though the Cavalier is a highly social breed, it is still important to get him out and about as a young puppy so that he can get used to all kinds of people, animals, noises, and sights. It may be difficult if you live in an urban area such as New York City, where there is worry about disease, and vets often ask owners to keep their puppy inside until fully vaccinated. A puppy class might be the way to go if you worry about taking your puppy out without being fully vaccinated. If you live in the suburbs or country where you might feel safer, take him to a small shopping mall and walk up and down or to a puppy play area. Take him with you when you go to the pet store to buy dog food. Puppy classes are great even for those puppies who do get to go out and about.

CRATE TRAINING

Crate training is the process of training your dog to accept his crate as a safe and calm place. A crate will help with housetraining, keep him safe from chewing on dangerous objects when you are too busy to keep a close eye on him, and offer him a safe place to go when he wants to be alone. For some anxious dogs, the crate may be seen as the place in which they feel most secure and may offer a feeling of calm.

Dogs are natural "den" animals, so a crate is far from cruel. If you do not have a crate for your

PUPPY POINTER

While your Cavalier is a puppy, put him onto a table from time to time. Remember, he will go onto a table every time he goes to the vet and/or groomer (if you choose to have someone else groom your Cavalier), so it will help to get him used to being on a table.

Cavalier, he will create his own den. It might be under the corner end table, crammed into the corner of the couch, behind the toilet, or somewhere enclosed and protected. If you use a crate properly, your puppy will see his crate just as a human teenager sees his own bedroom: as a place to stay when he wishes to rest or not be disturbed.

Besides for housetraining, the crate is great to use when you are gone from the house because it prevents a puppy from getting into mischief—chewing on electrical cords, couches, cushions, floors, and even walls! As your puppy proves himself capable of being left in the house loose without chewing things up and getting into things, you can start leaving him out for longer and longer periods.

CRATE SIZE

A good crate size for a Cavalier is 18 by 24 inches (45.5 by 61 cm) or 21 by 30 inches (53.5 by 76 cm)—bigger is not better. It should be large enough for an adult Cavalier to lie down, spread out comfortably, stand up fully, and turn around

Your Cavalier's crate will be his place of refuge when he wants to be left alone.

without difficulty. For a young puppy it is a good idea to have a crate divider that can be used to make the crate temporarily much smaller. It should be small so as not to encourage him to soil in one corner and still be able to lie down in another corner. Older dogs do prefer the more den-like enclosed-sided crates, but it might be best to use a wire crate for young puppies. This way you can easily keep a close eye on your dog while in the crate. You'll be able to see when he is sleeping and awake and even when he is acting as though he wants to go outside.

HOW TO CRATE TRAIN

Keep the crate near the door where your puppy is to go outside to go potty. This will help him learn your routine more quickly. If you want him to sleep next to your bed, either move the crate back and forth each morning and night or buy a second crate to keep in your bedroom.

If you bought your puppy from a responsible breeder, he will already be used to a crate. If not, you may need to get him used to it. Use treats and short periods of time in the crate at first, lengthening the time as your puppy becomes accustomed to it. Start slowly, enticing him into the crate with a treat and praising him when he goes inside. When he willingly walks in and out of the crate all the time, place him inside with a treat and a sturdy toy for him to play with and chew, and close the door. Let him stay for several minutes, and then let him out, praising him only at that time. Slowly expand the time he is in the crate with the door shut. If he complains by crying and/or barking, use a sharp "No!" to get him to stop. Your puppy must understand that he is not to make noise while in the crate. Do not use reassuring words or phrases if he cries because he needs to learn that the crate is his quiet place. At most a quick "Good puppy!" when he has been quiet for a bit will suffice. I have found that about one-third of all puppies will make no noise at all the first night in their new home, about one-third will make a bit of noise for a few days, and the rest will cry for about a week before settling in. If your puppy is still crying after a week, make sure that you are not encouraging him to make noise by talking to him.

Once he is no longer chewing or getting into things while you are home, start leaving him out while you make a quick run to the store or pick up your children from school. If he proves himself after a month or two of this, start leaving him when you go to the grocery store or wherever. As he proves himself more and more capable, you can lengthen his time uncrated until he no longer needs to be shut up in it at all.

Always leave his crate available to him, however. As mentioned earlier, it will be his place of refuge when he wants to be left alone.

The key to housetraining is to get your Cavalier puppy to consider your entire house as his den, which he will naturally want to keep clean.

HOUSETRAINING

A Cavalier puppy is capable of holding his urine for about as long as one hour for every month that he is old. This means that a two-month-old puppy is usually capable of holding his urine about two hours, a three-month-old about three hours, and so on until four or five months of age. By that time most puppies will be able to hold their urine all night long and up to eight hours during the day—especially when they are eating only one or two meals a day.

The key to housetraining is to get your Cavalier puppy to consider your entire house as his den. Puppies do not like to soil their den if they have been raised properly in clean surroundings. This is why you need to close off most of the crate at first so that your puppy cannot soil in one corner of his crate and still rest comfortably in another corner. It will take some time for him to get the notion that your huge house (huge to him!) is to be considered his den.

The best way to instill this idea is to make sure that he never gets the chance to potty in your home. If he is always going potty outside, it won't take long at all for him to recognize your entire home as his den and that he should always keep it "clean." If he occasionally goes potty inside, it will take longer. This is why pee pads are not such a good idea—if you use them, you are literally teaching your puppy to pee in his den. Unfortunately, puppy mill and pet shop puppies tend to be raised in dirty conditions and have become used to peeing and pooping in their den and walking through their own filth. They are likely to take longer to potty train.

HOW TO HOUSETRAIN

The first week you bring your puppy home, try to keep him off your floor constantly, except for a few minutes right after he has peed and pooped outside. Remember, this puppy has never soiled your house, so try to keep it that way! He should be outside, in his crate, in your arms, or on your lap—anywhere but the floor that first week or so—so that he doesn't have the opportunity to potty indoors. During this week he will be getting used to your routine, learning about you, learning about the door to go outside to go potty, and becoming used to your water and possibly your new food. At the same time you will be learning about your puppy, seeing his body language, watching what he does before peeing or pooping, and learning all the signals he gives. Most puppies will begin to run in erratic circles, occasionally sniffing the floor or ground looking for just the right place to potty or may even start digging motions. Some very smart puppies may run to a window or door almost immediately. Other puppies, especially those who may be less assertive, may give nearly undetectable signals, but nearly all will act a bit more active or anxious.

Always take your puppy out the same door (and accompany him outside) every time so that he learns that this is the door to go to. Another suggestion that seems to work well for older, nearly housetrained puppies and for busy people is to buy a bell that has a loud ring and tie it to the doorknob of the door your puppy goes through to go outside. Tie it low enough so that he hits it when he goes near the door, even accidentally while playing. *Every* time he rings the bell, drop everything, come running instantly, and take him outside. If he goes potty, praise him enthusiastically; if he doesn't within a minute or two, bring him back inside and go about your business. If the bell rings again, run. In

When your puppy potties successfully outdoors, praise him and offer an occasional treat.

a very short period, he will understand that the ring of the bell brings him instant attention, and he'll soon make the association between the ring of the bell and going potty.

HOUSETRAINING ACCIDENTS

If your puppy potties in the house, do not verbally correct him unless you catch him in the act of eliminating—not when finishing up but right before or while he's peeing or pooping. If you do catch him in the act, grab him and run outdoors—do not wait until he is done going potty. While you are running him outside, say "No, no, no, potty outside!" several times, stressing the word "outside." Once outside, put your puppy down and keep saying "Go potty" (or whatever words you want to use—some people like "Hurry up.") If you get lucky and there is any potty left and your puppy goes, praise, praise, praise! When you use simple words and one- or two-word phrases, your puppy will quickly learn what those words actually mean. This will help housetrain him much more quickly.

COMMON HOUSETRAINING MISTAKES

The following are the three biggest reasons for housetraining failure:

#1: Too Much Freedom

The number-one biggest mistake is letting your puppy have too much

Dog Tale

Many Cavaliers do very well in obedience and agility. They are not as active or as fast as some other breeds so may not "wow" the audience with their performance, but they are similar in trainability and may even be as smart as or smarter than some of those fast-moving, high-scoring breeds. My first Cavalier, Lawmaker, was the second in the history of the breed to obtain the level of Utility Dog. He often proved himself to be highly intelligent. One day he surprised the whole class by being the first to figure out how to retrieve his dumbbell from under a chair with a lot of rungs. Every other dog kept sticking his head in this way and that way trying to grab the dumbbell to no avail, but not Lawmaker. He ran to the chair and never stuck his head in once! Instead, what he did was take his paw and swipe the dumbbell out from under the chair, grabbed it with his mouth, and ran back to me as if he had done it every day of his life!

Give your dog positive feedback when he successfully potties outside.

unsupervised freedom in the house. Don't let him have any unsupervised freedom at first. Do whatever it takes to keep a close eye on him at all times for those first few weeks. The idea is to completely prevent him from soiling in your home—ever—and even more so to successfully have him always potty outside so that he realizes that outside is the only place he should do his business. This will help instill in him the notion that your entire home is his den.

#2: Bad Timing

The number-two biggest mistake is punishing your puppy (in the form of a verbal correction only, of course; you should never punish him physically) at the wrong time. Timing is so critical that it may be better to never punish him for going potty in your house. If you can't correct him while he's in the act of pottying indoors, punishment will only cause him to think that you occasionally go crazy for no reason at all. It is better to reward your puppy only when he goes potty outside. Dogs live so in the moment that they haven't a clue why you are angry for finding a potty mistake five minutes after it was left. That look your Cavalier gives you when you reprimand him after the fact? It's fear, not guilt!

#3: No Positive Feedback

The number-three biggest mistake is letting your puppy pee outside with no positive feedback. If you do not see him going potty outside and do not praise him for doing so, he won't know that he is doing the right thing. Go outside with him while he potties, but be all business. Do not talk to him or play with him—simply take him outside and be there, occasionally using your potty words ("Go potty" or Hurry up"). As soon as he pees and/or poops, praise him and give him a treat. Then you can play with him or go back inside.

BASIC OBEDIENCE

Obedience training is the process of teaching a dog basic manners. A trained dog is easier to live with, take for a walk, or take for a visit to a friend or the vet. When done correctly, it also uses the dog's natural instincts and helps cement his place in your family, all of which lead to a dog who is more confident, calm, and happy.

Basic obedience training is the process of teaching a dog good manners.

SIT

The *sit* is one of the most basic commands. It is one of the easiest to learn and helps instill a type of respect for the dog's owner/trainer. It can also be used as a means to calm a dog who is anxious and/or excited. Once the *sit* is learned, it is easier to go on to learn more difficult commands.

How to Teach It

The best way to teach the *sit* may be to capture the behavior; in other words, wait for him to sit on his own and then click (or use your marker word) and treat. Once your puppy is sitting for the treat, start using the word "sit." Using a clicker is such a wonderful way to teach the *sit*—there's no jerking on the collar, no pushing the rump down—nothing but positive training.

A more common method is to lure your dog into position. Have him in front of you, and with a treat, slowly move it from in front of him to up and over his head. As he follows the treat up with his eyes, he will naturally sit to remain stable.

Once he is almost sitting, say "Sit" one time and then when he is fully sitting, praise him and give him the treat.

Remember not to use your dog's name with any stationary command because he will want to go to you when he hears his name—not sit or stay. He will probably become confused if you do use his name with a stationary command.

COME (RECALL)

The *recall* is an absolute necessity for your puppy to learn and may even be a lifesaver if you need him to immediately come to you to escape a dangerous situation.

How to Teach It

The first rule of the *recall* is to never, ever call your puppy to you unless you can say "Fido, come" one time and then make sure that he comes to you immediately. Once he is completely trained and always comes to you while on a long leash, you can start taking chances and give him a *come* command when you aren't able to "make" him do it immediately by reeling him in on the leash. If you're training the *recall* indoors, use a shorter lead (see Chapter 3) to prevent it from getting caught on things and just let him drag it around.

At various times during the day when your puppy's leash is within reach,

Do not attempt a recall without a leash unless your dog is coming quickly every single time you call him.

suddenly say "Fido, come" while grabbing the leash and start to move backward so that he runs toward you. The moment he is next to you, praise effusively and release him. Do this for several weeks. Do not attempt a *recall* without the leash unless your puppy is coming quickly every single time you call him.

If you happen to call your puppy while not on leash and he doesn't respond, say nothing further. Go get a leash immediately, or get close enough to your puppy that you can grab his leash if it is on him and do a quickie training session on the *recall* right then and there. Do not wait or he will have learned that he can get away with not responding. Puppies are just like children—if they can get away with it once, they will think that they can get away with it again.

Please note that the use of the word "come" should be limited to either training times when you are positive that you can reinforce the command or at other times when you are positive that your dog will come on the first command. If there is ever a question of whether your puppy will respond, such as when he is playing outside and you are getting ready to leave and want to call him in, use his name only to get his attention. This will prevent him from associating the *come* command with something he perceives as negative—the cessation of his playtime.

If your puppy doesn't come when you call his name, do not chase him or you will be teaching him to run away. This includes following him at a slower pace—he'll still see it as a game. The best thing to do is to call out his name, and when he looks your way, start running in the opposite direction. Most of the time your puppy will follow you, and in fact, when he feels that he isn't in control, he will actually try to outrun you. So head back to where you want him to go, and chances are he will try to beat you there! However, it's best that your puppy never be free outside in an unfenced area until he is totally trustworthy.

As a final note, never, ever correct your dog when he comes to you, no matter how long it took or how many commands you may have inadvertently given before he responded. If you do you are teaching him that he will be punished when he comes to you, and he will learn to avoid it. Always reward him for coming to you, no matter what the circumstances are, and you will teach him that coming to you is an enjoyable event.

DOWN

Down is one of the hardest things to teach a dog, especially a younger one. This is a submissive behavior that takes some confidence for a puppy to comfortably perform. Your Cavalier will need lots of praise while learning this command.

How to Teach It

When your puppy is sitting, use a treat to lure his nose lower and in a forward direction until his elbows have touched the ground and he is lying on the floor. You may use your other hand to keep him from moving forward. Again, don't use your puppy's name with this command

BE AWARE!
Start training the moment you get your puppy home. Don't allow bad habits to develop simply because he is so cute!

Your Cavalier will need lots of praise while learning the *down* command.

because it is a stationary cue. Also, don't click and treat until he is all the way on the floor—elbows and all. Use lots of praise and other positive reinforcement so that your puppy feels comfortable and not threatened.

STAY

The *stay* is used in many aspects of daily living. One of the most important reasons to teach this cue is to keep your dog from running out of your house every time you open the door. It can also be a big help for you, your dog's veterinarian, and the groomer during procedures in which he needs to stay still, such as cutting his nails or taking his temperature. Like the *sit*, this is another command that may also help calm your dog when he is overly excited.

How to Teach It

Once your puppy is sitting or lying down, go ahead and praise him, but wait longer and longer to give him a treat so that he remains in that same position for progressively longer periods. Start saying the word "stay," drawing the word out slowly: "Staaaayy." This will calm your dog and help prevent him from getting excited and moving. Make sure that the command sounds as if you mean it, not as

Even adult Cavaliers benefit from refresher obedience training.

if you are mildly requesting him to stay. Again, don't use his name or he may think that he is being called and may start to jump up.

When your puppy is consistently staying, start to step in front of him first before rewarding; then slowly move farther and farther away from him before clicking, treating, and releasing. By slowly, this means step in front of your puppy for several training sessions, then 1 foot (0.5 m) away for several training sessions, then 5 feet (1.5 m) away for several training sessions, and so on. This does not mean to move farther and farther away in the very first training session! Take teaching this cue nice and slowly.

HEEL (WALK NICELY ON LEASH)

All dogs should be trained to heel. The *heel* command will train your dog to keep more of his attention on you rather than his surroundings, which will calm him, help him feel more secure, and keep him from straining ahead, causing his owner to have sore arms or even trip and fall. A dog who has been trained to heel also contributes to safer and more enjoyable walks and visits.

How to Teach It

From day one, don't let your puppy pull on the leash—ever. There is nothing worse than seeing a dog taking his owner for a walk, straining forward every step of the way. Use a clicker and treats to keep your puppy in the right position: right shoulder area at your left leg. Praise, click, and treat whenever he walks with you in that correct position, and stop moving when he's not. Note that the treat may also be used as a lure by holding it so that your puppy is walking in the correct position, attempting to get the treat. Whenever he has been walking calmly for a bit in the correct position, you may feed him the treat and begin again with a new one.

A puppy who is determined to plunge ahead can also be controlled by unexpectedly changing your direction often so that he doesn't know what is going to happen next and begins to keep a better eye on you. As soon as he begins to plunge ahead, make an abrupt about-turn, talking positively to him with a very happy voice, saying "Fido, heel." As soon as he "catches back up" and is where he should be, click, treat, and praise once again. Because the *heel* is a moving command, it's fine and actually preferable to use your puppy's name each time you say the cue to get his attention.

FINDING AN OBEDIENCE CLASS

Most breed clubs have puppy classes, which are for puppies about four months to eight months of age. These classes include lots of socialization and some beginning obedience. Choose an upbeat class and an instructor with positive training methods.

When your puppy is close to a year of age, he is ready for more formal obedience training. Hopefully you will have already laid out some initial groundwork. Again, most breed clubs have obedience classes, and so do many pet stores. Attending classes is sometimes better than bringing in a professional trainer because *you* are the one who needs most of the training!

FINDING A PROFESSIONAL TRAINER

To find a professional trainer, look online, ask your vet, or call various breed clubs—most of them know a few good professional trainers. Often your breeder can do just as good a job as a professional trainer if the breeder lives in your area. A professional trainer should obviously love dogs, have a patient, firm, and calm manner, use positive training methods, and heavily involve the dog's owner (you!) in many of the training sessions.

Professional trainers can be very helpful, but remember that most of the training is up to you. To achieve long-term success, you must continue the training once the professional has left.

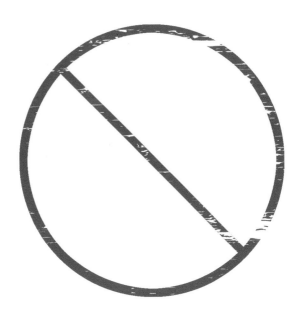

SOLVING PROBLEMS WITH YOUR CAVALIER KING CHARLES SPANIEL

A well-behaved Cavalier is a pleasure to take out and about.

Your dog is always watching you and learning from your behavior and body language. You are always teaching him. If he is not doing what you want him to do, evaluate your own actions carefully. It is almost a given that you are inadvertently training him to do exactly what he is doing wrong! It often helps to figure out what it is *you* are doing wrong and take steps to fix it.

Owning a dog is a choice and will entail a lifestyle change from the very first day. Dogs live in the immediate moment, so timing is important. A correction made even seconds after the wrong behavior is a correction made too late. It's better to not correct at all than to correct at the wrong time, as you will only confuse your dog further and create more problems.

Listed below are various problems that can be created or that you may have inherited if you adopted a rescued or older Cavalier. Some solutions to those problems will be listed as well, including ways in which you can alter your behavior or that of your dog. Owning a pet should be a thoroughly joyful experience, not an unhappy one. If your dog is creating stress in your family, it is time to step back and make some changes!

BARKING

Barking is a very natural dog behavior—it's a dog's way of communicating. Dogs will bark for attention, to go outside, for food or water, or possibly when anxious or frightened. It is also a behavior that can simply become a habit if allowed to go on for too long, and that's when it becomes a problem.

Start when your puppy is very young if possible, and stop any and all inappropriate barking the second it starts. If you let the barking happen too often, allow it to become a habit, or let it occur at inappropriate times, it will become annoying. Now is the time to take steps to stop excessive barking.

SOLUTION

Make sure that you don't give your dog attention by making soothing noises or words while he's barking. If you do you will be teaching him that it is okay to bark because it is getting him the attention he is demanding.

If your Cavalier is barking because he is anxious, he may actually need more crate time. Please don't put the crate away when your dog is potty trained. Why would you take it away? Dogs are natural den animals, so he will see his den as his happy place as well as his secure place—his own "bedroom" and sanctuary. It is his place to go if he is not feeling well or if he is anxious or just wants to be alone, so do not let children play with or antagonize him while he is in there. If he starts barking while in his crate, he wants something. He may need water or a potty break or more attention. It is fine to give him water if he needs it or to take him outside if he needs to potty. And certainly, your Cavalier deserves plenty of attention, but teach him to not need it *all* the time. If you know that you are giving your Cavalier plenty of attention and he still wants more, simply ignore his attention-getting actions. It may help to vary the time you feed him or play with him so that he learns that you will do so when *you* decide to, not when he asks.

BE AWARE!

If you don't want your adult Cavalier to do something such as get on the couch or jump up to greet you, make him aware that those things are forbidden the first day you bring him home. Don't confuse him by letting him do those things because he is a cute little puppy when you know that he won't be allowed to do them later.

If something is causing his barking, such as seeing something through the window, you might want to eliminate his ability to see through that window. If he is often barking when outside alone, bring him inside so that it doesn't become a habit.

If your Cavalier's barking becomes a problem or especially if it has become a bad habit, one possible solution is to teach him how to "speak" on command. In other words, train him to "speak" by reinforcing his barking with the word "speak" and rewarding him only when he barks immediately after you have given the command. Once he has learned how, you can teach him the *quiet* command by doing the opposite. As soon as he becomes quiet, say "Quiet" and reward if he remains quiet for a few seconds.

CHEWING

Dogs are natural chewers. If allowed complete freedom, most dogs would spend a great

Give your puppy plenty of appropriate chew items instead of allowing him to chew inappropriate or even potentially dangerous things.

deal of time each day chewing. Chewing is natural and good for them, but when he is living in your house you do not want your Cavalier to chew on inappropriate items such as furniture and footwear. The more active your dog and/or the more intelligent, the more likely he is to get bored easily and need to chew.

SOLUTION

The best thing to do is to never allow your puppy to chew anything of yours. If you do not want him to chew on your shoes, for example, don't let him chew *any* shoes—not even your old ones. How is he supposed to know the difference? Also, give him plenty of appropriate chew items such as safe bones and toys. If your puppy is especially active or you let him have too much unsupervised time and he chews inappropriate items, he might become a problem chewer. To prevent that development, step in and take control.

Go back to the beginning. Whenever you are unable to watch your Cavalier closely, put him into his crate and give him appropriate chew items. Don't give him the opportunity to gain access to anything you don't want him to chew. If he starts to chew something inappropriate, put him directly into his crate with an appropriate chew item and close the door. Let him out when you are able to keep a close eye on him. If he appears bored, find some things for him to do to get his mind off chewing. Remember, dogs are not statues! They need some of your time every single day. A dog who is never allowed to chew inappropriate items does not think of chewing them when given a little more freedom. And always remember that it is a good idea to praise your Cavalier when you find him chewing on an appropriate item. Encourage his good behavior!

All puppies go through a chewing stage when they are teething. Supply your puppy with good things to chew during this stage. A great idea to try is to freeze baby carrots and give your puppy one now and then. He can chew on the carrot, the coldness will soothe sore gums, and he will be getting a bit of good nutrition as well.

DIGGING

Dogs love to dig for a variety of reasons. Some will try to dig out of their yard when they hear or smell something interesting, sometimes just for something to do, or sometimes because they want to visit a human or animal friend. Some do it for pure enjoyment—kind of like how some people enjoy working out. Some will dig to bury a treasure or dig to get it back out. Luckily, most Cavaliers are not avid diggers. They may dig now and then, but they rarely do it to the extent that many other breeds do. But if your Cavalier is digging, you need to figure out why.

If your Cavalier is trying to dig out of your yard, he may be spending too much time alone outside and may be bored.

SOLUTION

If your Cavalier is trying to dig out of your yard, he may be spending too much time alone outside and may be bored. One obvious way to stop this is to not leave him outside for long periods. This breed should spend the vast majority of its time indoors.

If you have a doggy door and your Cavalier has the freedom to go outside at will, you may have to take preventive measures. Make digging a fruitless activity. Line the edge of the yard with bushes so that your Cavalier cannot get close enough to the fence to think about digging out. If you have an especially avid explorer, you might need to put something under the fence or line the edge with patio blocks to prevent him from digging out. If your Cavalier is trying to go after a critter he saw, limit his time outside and keep him away from that area until he forgets about it. If the critter actually lives in your yard, the smell will never go away and you might have to bring in an exterminator. If your dog appears to be digging for the pleasure of it, give him a place to dig. Choose a corner of the yard and build something akin to a sandbox. Bury treats in it so that he will be drawn to that area.

HOUSE SOILING

Nothing is worse than having a dog who still potties in your house from time to time. Not only is this not clean and will eventually cause your house to smell, but you won't be very happy with your Cavalier if you can't trust him to potty outdoors. Your puppy should be fairly reliable in the housetraining area by four months of age. If not, it is time to take more serious measures.

SOLUTION

First make sure that your puppy is physically okay. Some exceptionally tiny puppies or those with especially rounded heads who could be a bit hydrocephalic may be physically and mentally more immature. They might take more time to gain good control. Your puppy could have a bladder infection as well. Have him evaluated by a vet, and if all is fine, start looking at your training methods. Remember to not

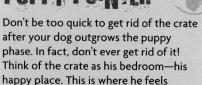

PUPPY POINTER

Don't be too quick to get rid of the crate after your dog outgrows the puppy phase. In fact, don't ever get rid of it! Think of the crate as his bedroom—his happy place. This is where he feels secure, and you can use it as a training tool for the rest of his life.

allow your puppy much freedom until he is completely trained. Don't allow "mistakes" to happen. If all else fails, the following technique should do the trick. If done properly I have yet to see it fail.

With this technique you basically set your puppy up to "fail"— to go potty in your house—but maintain complete control over the situation by giving him your undivided attention. Choose a smaller room in your house—maybe a bedroom—a room that doesn't have many places where he will not be visible. After your puppy has been in his crate for a period of time and you know that he will need to pee, get him out of his crate and take him to that room and close the door. Put him on the floor, sit down on the bed or a chair, and pretend that you are reading a book. Keep a *very* close eye on your puppy every single second and do not do anything else. Do not interact with him. He will run around for a bit exploring but will soon decide that he has to pee. Remember, you are watching your puppy intently the whole time, not taking your eyes off him for even one second. You will see his every movement, and you will easily see when he decides to squat and pee. Because he was in his crate for some time, he will need to pee quickly. Be completely alert, and the second your puppy starts to squat, pick him up (you might want to put your hand underneath in case he is still peeing, so it might be a good idea if you are wearing a vinyl glove at this time) and run him outside, sternly saying "Ah, ah, ah, potty outside." (Note that you should have been saying "Outside" when your puppy went outside and saying "Inside" when he went back into the house all along so that he knows what inside and outside mean.) While running outside, keep repeating "Ah, ah, ah, potty outside." Put your puppy down outside, and if you are lucky and he has any potty left and pees, praise him effusively. This technique is also a way to get you to learn proper timing. It is the rare puppy indeed who experiences five of these "intense" training sessions and doesn't finally get it.

If your Cavalier is getting old and after many years of being housetrained suddenly starts having accidents, a veterinary checkup may be needed. Some of the housetraining lapses may be unavoidable, although there are some hormonally based drugs that may help a bit. Cavaliers with advanced mitral valve disease (MVD) may need to take a medication that causes them to drink a lot more water, which in turn causes them to pee a lot more, so you may start seeing some accidents from this as well. Thankfully, most dogs eventually adjust to the medication and regain their housetraining.

JUMPING UP

This is a cute behavior as a puppy that can become a problem behavior when your Cavalier gets older. Even a small dog can knock over a small child or fragile adult. It may be best to not allow your puppy to ever jump up and thus prevent the creation of a habit. It is hard to resist being greeted by that cute puppy, though! In all honesty, I allow my own Cavaliers to jump up to greet visitors and just crate them if small children or fragile adults visit. It may be because I show my dogs and want them eager to greet everyone. This has not caused a problem so far. But if you have a baby who is soon to become a toddler or a fragile parent who's visiting, you may need to teach your Cavalier to stop jumping up in greeting.

SOLUTION

One of the best ways to deal with jumping up is to teach your Cavalier what the word "off" means. Whenever your Cavalier starts to jump up on you, tell him "Off" and gently put your leg out to prevent him from getting near you. The reason he jumps up is to get nearer, and if he cannot do so he will back off and get back down on all fours. If you do this consistently, he will soon learn that the word "off" means just that—to get off you and back down on his own four legs. Once you have taught him the *off* command, you can use it whenever he is starting to jump up to greet someone.

MOUTHING/NIPPING

Mouthing and nipping are just part of the natural chewing habit that dogs have. Puppies also like to mouth things just as human babies do. They learn a lot from this behavior. It is annoying only when it becomes excessive or your puppy begins to mouth or "bite" too hard. A puppy who has never learned bite inhibition is more likely to turn into an adult who may bite hard enough to injure someone.

SOLUTION

Teach your puppy bite inhibition. He learned a lot by play biting his littermates, but you need to continue teaching him. This means that you need to allow him to mouth and "bite" your fingers, but the second he starts to use too much force and it feels the least bit uncomfortable, say "Owwww" firmly and somewhat loudly. If your puppy bites down even harder, the "Owwww" should get even louder until he backs off. This teaches him to know his own strength and can prevent more problems down the road. Everyone in your family should use this technique. Over time get even more "sensitive" and yell "Owwww" at lighter and lighter pressures until your puppy ceases the behavior altogether.

PULLING ON LEAD

Cavaliers are so cute when they are little puppies. They are very friendly and

quite small when you first bring them home. When such a tiny puppy charges ahead enthusiastically on leash to visit everything and everyone, it's easy to be enchanted and forget that you are letting him start a bad habit.

SOLUTION

No matter how cute your puppy appears, don't allow him to pull on the lead. If you allow him to pull even sometimes, you will be teaching him that it is okay to do so whenever he wants.

Every time your puppy starts to charge ahead or pull, quickly turn direction so that he learns to look to you. Do this repeatedly until he is not forging ahead. I do not suggest using a harness with a puppy until he is completely and totally leash

Proper leash behavior is a cornerstone of good training.

trained and does not pull. The fit of a harness seems to encourage pulling, so it is not a good lead-training item. Don't forget that dogs are very good at reading body language, so teach your Cavalier to always look to you for guidance. This will help in *all* areas, not just in preventing lead pulling.

SEPARATION ANXIETY

Separation anxiety is a condition in which a dog develops anxiety whenever separated from his owner. He may bark or whine excessively, chew on inappropriate items, or pace continuously back and forth. Creating a big fuss when you leave and especially when you arrive home is the main reason for separation anxiety in dogs. If your Cavalier develops this condition, it is time to start over and change your arrival and departure routines.

SOLUTION

The best thing to do is to make leaving and arriving normal events—in other words, keep them as low-key as possible. Whenever you depart the house, place your puppy in his crate without fuss and leave. He will be happier in the security of his den. Once you begin to allow him out of his crate when you leave home, put him back in there if he shows any anxiety at all. Don't allow the anxiety to take hold. Whenever you arrive home, ignore your puppy for a bit of time—sometimes for just 1 minute, sometimes for 5 minutes, sometimes for 15 minutes—change it around all the time. Then let him outside to potty and after that play with him for a bit. Act as though leaving and coming home are totally natural and nothing to get excited about—or to even think about. If you do this, your puppy should soon see your comings and goings that way too.

If none of these methods work, it is time to seek professional help. A good behaviorist may be your best option.

SOUND SENSITIVITY

Some dogs are afraid of loud noises such as thunder, lightning, and fireworks. Whenever there is a thunderstorm or fireworks are going off, a Cavalier with a noise phobia might cling to your side, shivering and shaking or hiding under the bed.

SOLUTION

Your dog's crate should be his place of comfort. Sometimes just putting him inside his crate will work. He will feel more secure there and settle down. Try not to make soothing sounds because this may cause him to believe that there really is something wrong. Also, make sure that you are not transmitting your own fears to your dog—remember how good dogs are with interpreting body language! If

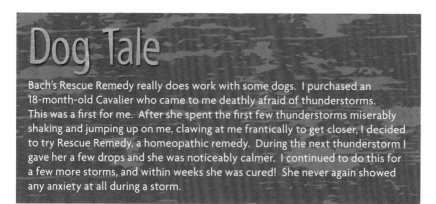

Dog Tale

Bach's Rescue Remedy really does work with some dogs. I purchased an 18-month-old Cavalier who came to me deathly afraid of thunderstorms. This was a first for me. After she spent the first few thunderstorms miserably shaking and jumping up on me, clawing at me frantically to get closer, I decided to try Rescue Remedy, a homeopathic remedy. During the next thunderstorm I gave her a few drops and she was noticeably calmer. I continued to do this for a few more storms, and within weeks she was cured! She never again showed any anxiety at all during a storm.

A professional trainer or behaviorist can really make a difference in a dog's life..

you are afraid of thunderstorms, it is quite likely your Cavalier will pick up on it and become afraid as well.

Sometimes giving a dog a few drops of Bach's Rescue Remedy, a homeopathic remedy that works to calm dogs, can help. It also works on humans too! You can find it online or at health stores. If your Cavalier is truly miserable, you may need to get something stronger from your vet.

There are CDs you can play to desensitize your dog to loud noises. They start out with the noises at a lower level and get increasingly louder and louder so that your dog can gradually get used to the sound. Please refer to the Bibliography for places to order one of these CDs.

WHEN TO SEEK PROFESSIONAL HELP

If you have moments when you wish you didn't have your dog and it is due to his behavior (or misbehavior), it is probably time to seek professional help. If your dog embarrasses you from time to time, it is probably time to seek professional help. If you are struggling with training and either you and/or your dog doesn't seem to know what to do, it is time to seek professional help. If your friends or neighbors no longer want to visit because of your dog, or your dog is beginning to exhibit a dangerous behavior such as aggression, it is truly time to seek professional help.

You can look for behaviorists in your area in a phone book or online. Your vet probably knows of a few, and your Cavalier's breeder may be able to help as well. Most area breed clubs know names of the best behaviorists in the area. Try not to wait too long. You don't want to wait until something is an ingrained habit before seeking help. Habits are hard to break—just think about how hard it is for you to break your own long-standing habits!

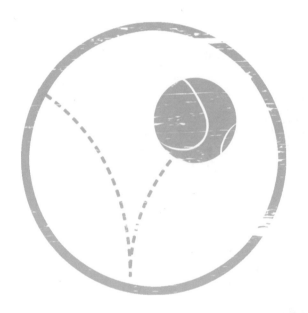

ACTIVITIES WITH YOUR CAVALIER KING CHARLES SPANIEL

Dog agility is a sport in which a handler directs the dog through an obstacle course in a race for both time and accuracy.

C avaliers are a very social breed and naturally people oriented, but if you'd like to create an even closer bond, you may want to try additional activities with your pet. A Cavalier is usually willing to try almost anything as long as he gets to spend more time with you.

SPORTS AND ACTIVITIES

Cavaliers tend to be sporty, athletic, intelligent, and eager to please, making them an easy breed to train and perform in many different activities. These characteristics contribute to making the Cavalier one of the very best breeds of all suited to therapy work. They are also the number-two toy breed in numbers gaining titles in both obedience and agility events. Not only does a Cavalier do well in these activities, but they tend to be so enthusiastic about it, it would almost be a shame to not let your Cavalier participate in at least one of these events.

AGILITY

Dog agility is a sport in which a handler directs the dog through an obstacle course in a race for both time and accuracy. The dog runs off leash with no food or toys as incentives, and the handler is not allowed to touch the dog or the obstacles. Control is limited to voice, movement, and various body signals, which requires exceptional training of the dog and coordination with his handler.

Agility is an extremely fun sport for both the dog and handler. In the American Kennel Club (AKC) there are three levels of agility, from Novice through Excellent, with each level getting progressively more difficult. Dogs with the Excellent title may continue to compete for points toward their Master Agility Championship (MACH) title and add more levels of MACH for as long as they continue to compete. The AKC also offers classes in Jumpers and Weaves. Additional organizations also offer competitive agility. Most of them offer other types of classes in addition to the standard agility, keeping the sport varied and interesting.

Please make sure that your Cavalier is sound before attempting agility. This sport involves a great deal of jumping, twisting, running, and other strenuous activities that you don't want to subject your dog to if there is any evidence of skeletal problems. Competing in agility can damage a dog who is unsound, so be sure to test for hip dysplasia, patellar luxation, and other skeletal problems before doing agility with your Cavalier. Also, although it may be fun to do a little bit of agility with your puppy, don't start formal agility training and competing until he is fully mature—18 to 24 months—to prevent damage to undeveloped bones, joints, and muscles and other tissues.

CANINE GOOD CITIZEN® (CGC) PROGRAM

The Canine Good Citizen Program started in 1989 and is a certification program sponsored by the AKC designed to reward dogs who have good manners at home and in public. The program stresses responsible pet ownership and basic good manners for dogs.

PUPPY POINTER

Do not let your Cavalier puppy participate in performance events. Wait until he is 18 to 24 months of age and has been fully tested with regard to skeletal health. Puppies are simply not mature enough to safely participate, and some Cavaliers will never be sound enough.

The program consists of a test containing the following ten exercises: 1.) accepting a friendly stranger; 2.) sitting politely for petting; 3.) appearance and grooming; 4.) walking on a loose lead; 5.) walking through a crowd; 6.) sitting and downing on command/ staying in place; 7.) coming when called; 8.) reaction to another dog; 9.) reaction to distractions; and 10.) supervised separation from handler. The AKC gives a CGC certificate to dogs who pass this test.

CONFORMATION (DOG SHOWING)

Conformation is a beauty contest of sorts that compares how well a particular Cavalier meets the breed standard. Structure, movement, and temperament are important because all are considered part of the standard. Almost every country holds conformation shows. In the United States, Cavaliers can be shown in both the AKC and Cavalier King Charles Spaniel Club, USA, Inc. (CKCSC).

Conformation is a contest in which dogs are evaluated on how well they measure up to the breed standard.

Winning dogs are awarded points. The more dogs a Cavalier beats, the more points he can receive, up to a maximum of five points per show. To become a champion in the AKC, a dog has to have 15 points total, including 2 "majors." A dog is awarded a major if he beats enough dogs at a particular show to be awarded three points or more. In this way a dog cannot become a champion by beating just one, possibly inferior, dog at each show.

Cavaliers in the United States also have another choice. The original Cavalier club, the CKCSC (the original registry for the breed), has a large membership and many specialty shows each year all over the country that are well attended. CKCSC shows are judged similarly to the English Kennel Club. To get a CKCSC championship, your dog will need to beat other champions to gain points, which keeps the breed standard very high. If you want to see the best of the best, this is the place to go. For each weekend of shows there is a minimum of two shows in which to compete, so you can make a mini-vacation out of each show weekend. CKCSC shows are lots of fun.

FLYBALL

If your Cavalier loves to retrieve balls, flyball might be a good activity for him. Two teams at a time, each with four dogs, compete against each other and race over a course in relay form. Each dog must jump all of the jumps, press a lever that releases the ball, grab the ball, and return to his owner with it. As soon as he crosses the finish line, the next dog is released to run the course. The team to finish first without error wins that heat.

LURE COURSING

Another activity your Cavalier might like is lure coursing. A lure, usually a white piece of cloth, is attached to a line and pulled along the ground by a motor and pulley system. It is set up in a large field and moves just ahead of the dog who is chasing it. Although only recognized sighthounds can compete for titles, any breed of dog is eligible to participate for fun. Since most dogs enjoy chasing and the freedom of running at great speed, it is a lot of fun for them and a blast to watch. I have tried this with a couple of my Cavaliers and they loved it! If you have a very active Cavalier, this is a great way for him to get some good exercise and expend a lot of that excess energy.

Obedience aims to show that dogs can be trained to behave properly at all times.

OBEDIENCE

Obedience is a sport in which a dog must execute a predefined set of exercises when asked to do so by his handler as directed by a judge. These exercises are performed both on lead and off lead and consist of tasks such as heeling (both on and off lead), *recall*, a *sit-stay*, a *down-stay*, a stand for examination, retrieving, jumping, and various other exercises. The basic objective is to show that dogs can be trained to behave properly at all times. There are various levels of titles in the AKC, beginning with the Companion Dog (CD) title all the way through the Utility

Dog Excellent (UDX) and Obedience Trial Champion (OTCH). Each level gets progressively more difficult.

RALLY

Rally is a fairly new sport in which a handler and dog complete a course that has been designed by a judge. You proceed at your own pace through a course of 10 to 20 different stations, each of which has a sign providing instructions regarding the skill that is to be performed. You are permitted to talk, praise, encourage, clap your hands, pat your legs, or use any verbal means of encouragement to your dog. However, you may not touch your dog or make physical corrections.

The AKC offers three levels of rally:

- Novice, where all exercises such as *sit*, *stay*, *down*, *come*, and *heel* are performed on leash to demonstrate that the dog understands basic commands
- Advanced, which includes at least one jump and where the different exercises are performed off-leash
- Excellent, which is similar to Advanced, but the exercises are more difficult and demonstrate a higher level of skill for both dog and owner

Once your dog masters rally obedience, you may want to take the next step and participate in regular obedience.

THERAPY

When participating in therapy, you and your dog visit children and adults in hospitals and nursing homes. Your dog will visit patients and allow them to talk to him and pet him, providing comfort, companionship, and possibly a bit of physical therapy by getting patients to move their arms and hands while petting. To participate, your dog needs to be trained and certified according to the standards set by the specific sponsoring organization, such as Therapy Dogs International (TDI) or the Delta Society, the two main organizations in the United States.

Cavaliers are one of the very best breeds for therapy work because they are extremely people oriented and affectionate, are the

BE AWARE!
Whenever you travel with your Cavalier, bring a crate, small plastic bags, and cleanup supplies. Do your best to prevent accidents and always clean up after your Cavalier to ensure that dogs continue to be welcome at pet-friendly establishments.

Cavaliers are well suited to therapy work because they love people, are the perfect size, and have a gentle demeanor.

perfect size, and have a gentle demeanor and moderate activity level. Therapy work is very gratifying for dog, owner, and patients.

TRACKING

A dog is "tracking" when he follows the scent trail left by a human being (or other animal) that has passed along a certain route. Following a track is one of the many useful things dogs can do to help humans. Hounds track game, rescue dogs track lost children, police dogs track suspects, and well-trained pets can find lost items. Many dog owners are involved in tracking with their dogs as a hobby or as a sport (to earn titles), or both. Although they aren't scenthounds, there are a number of Cavaliers who have gained tracking titles. Some appear to have good noses and a real enjoyment of this sport.

There are three tracking titles available today, each progressively more complicated: Tracking Dog (TD), Tracking Dog Excellent (TDX), and Variable Surface Tracking (VST). For those dogs who have earned all three titles, the title of Champion Tracker (CT) is awarded.

If you and your Cavalier love being outdoors, this could be a wonderful sport for the two of you to try.

TRAVELING WITH YOUR CAVALIER

Cavaliers are delightful companions who love to go everywhere with their owners. They are so adaptable they rarely cause problems as long as you are prepared. So if you want to take your Cavalier along, please do! Here is how to prepare:

Cavaliers are delightful and adaptable travel companions.

- Always bring his crate along to sleep in and stay in whenever you are sleeping or not able to give him your undivided attention—even if and especially if you are staying with family or friends rather than in a hotel.
- Shortly before you leave, have your dog visit his veterinarian for a thorough checkup and get a signed health certificate. Keep the health certificate with you at all times.
- Bring along the following items: 1.) your dog's crate and bedding; 2.) health certificate with rabies tag/info; 3.) ID tags attached to collar—a microchip is even better; 4.) collar and leash; 5.) food; 6.) water from home or bottled water; 7.) towels in case you need to clean your pet; 8.) old sheets from home to cover beds in hotel if you are going to let your Cavalier climb up on them; 9.) cleaning supplies in case your dog has a potty accident; 10.) small plastic bags for outside cleanup; 11.) any medications your pet might be taking; and 12.) a first-aid kit for you and your family, as well as for your Cavalier.

TRAVELING BY CAR

If you are going to travel by car, make sure that your dog is secured in his crate or attached to a car harness whenever your vehicle is in motion.

Some dogs may get carsick. Some experience true motion sickness, while others experience it due to anxiety. Although both motion sickness and anxiety can be treated with medication, anxiety can usually be relieved by making sure that your dog goes for enjoyable car rides and not just to the vet. A visit to the vet is anxiety producing all by itself and can create carsickness in a dog who doesn't necessarily have motion sickness. Other dogs may experience less motion sickness as long as they can see out of the window. In most dogs, carsickness will eventually go away.

Finally, remember: Never leave your Cavalier alone in the car because he could become overheated, possibly fatally. A car can overheat very quickly even in moderate temperatures and with the windows open.

TRAVELING BY AIR

If you need to fly to your destination, you may still take your Cavalier along. Because the breed is small, you have two choices. Depending on the airline, you can put him in the cargo hold in his crate or take him on board in an approved soft-sided carrier and keep him right with you under the seat in front of you. Either way, he will need a current health certificate.

You will need to make a reservation for flying in advance, especially when taking your pet on board. Most airlines limit the number of on-board animals to two per flight, so you don't want your pet to be left out! There is a charge for taking your Cavalier along, and it isn't cheap. In fact, there may be times when your pet's ticket costs more than your own.

Most Cavaliers handle flying quite well.

LODGING

Find pet-friendly lodging before you leave on your trip. Nothing is worse than driving late into the night, getting more tired with every mile, and looking for a

Dog Tale

Cavaliers are such natural little dogs and take to almost any activity with ease. In my experience as a breeder, it is not at all unusual to sell a Cavalier to an individual who only wants one as a pet but ends up doing much more. There was one gentleman who had always wanted a Cavalier but waited to buy one until he had retired and had more time to devote to him. Some years later he discovered agility, and after several more years his dog had gained advanced agility titles. Another woman came to purchase her second pet Cavalier. Now she has two AKC/Canadian champions and is getting ready to breed her first litter! Never underestimate what you or your Cavalier can do.

When staying in a hotel, never allow your Cavalier on the bed unless it is covered.

hotel or motel that will accept both you and your pet. A simple online search for "pet-friendly hotels" will bring up dozens of sites that list this type of lodging by region, city, and/or state. You can also get guides from AAA and your local library.

Many hotels require a deposit for pets. Some will give your deposit back after a room check just before you leave, while others will not.

Always crate your Cavalier in your hotel room whenever you are sleeping or not in your room. Do not use hotel towels to bathe and dry your dog. Do not let your Cavalier on the beds unless they are covered. Minimize shedding on the carpeting. Clean flooring thoroughly should your Cavalier have an accident in the room. And always pick up after him outside. Be a responsible owner so that these types of hotels will continue to accept pets.

BOARDING

If you cannot take your Cavalier along, you will need to find a pet sitter or board him. Cavaliers are one of the most, if not *the* most, adaptable of all breeds and usually do well regardless of what choice you make.

Your breed club, friends, or your veterinarian may offer recommendations of good pet sitters in your area. A good pet sitter should love dogs, have a gentle but firm manner, and have some training experience. She should also have plans in place if an emergency arises with your pet. It is even better if she has some experience with your breed.

Should you decide to board your pet, again, get recommendations from a breed club, your friends, or your veterinarian. Plan an unannounced visit to suggested boarding kennels to check them out. Check out where your Cavalier will stay, how much outdoor time he will have, and how much individual attention he will get on a daily basis. Make sure that the employees are friendly, love dogs, and treat them with kindness. Also ensure that the kennel is clean and that there are no hazardous items your Cavalier could get into. In most cases, if your Cavalier is eager to go back the next time, you know that you have a winner.

If you are going to board your Cavalier and the kennel requires a current bordetella vaccination, get one about a month before you travel. (The bordetella vaccine is short-lived so should not be routinely given once a year.) If your trip happens nine months after your Cavalier was vaccinated, he may no longer have protection! This is one vaccination that should be given only when necessary and fairly close to the time of your trip.

Cavaliers enjoy
vacations too!

RESOURCES

ASSOCIATIONS AND ORGANIZATIONS

BREED CLUBS

American Cavalier King Charles Spaniel Club (ACKCS)
www.ackcsc.org

American Kennel Club (AKC)
5580 Centerview Drive
Raleigh, NC 27606
Telephone: (919) 233-9767
Fax: (919) 233-3627
E-Mail: info@akc.org
www.akc.org

Canadian Kennel Club (CKC)
89 Skyway Avenue, Suite 100
Etobicoke, Ontario M9W 6R4
Telephone: (416) 675-5511
Fax: (416) 675-6506
E-Mail: information@ckc.ca
www.ckc.ca

The Cavalier King Charles Spaniel Club-USA (CKCSC)
PO Box 330
Conway, NH 03818
Telephone : (603) 447-5218
Fax : (603) 447-5419
www.ckcsc.org

Federation Cynologique Internationale (FCI)
Secretariat General de la FCI
Place Albert 1er, 13
B – 6530 Thuin
Belqique
www.fci.be

The Kennel Club
1 Clarges Street
London
W1J 8AB
Telephone: 0870 606 6750
Fax: 0207 518 1058
www.the-kennel-club.org.uk

United Kennel Club (UKC)
100 E. Kilgore Road
Kalamazoo, MI 49002-5584
Telephone: (269) 343-9020
Fax: (269) 343-7037
E-Mail: pbickell@ukcdogs.com
www.ukcdogs.com

PET SITTERS

National Association of Professional Pet Sitters
15000 Commerce Parkway, Suite C
Mt. Laurel, New Jersey 08054
Telephone: (856) 439-0324
Fax: (856) 439-0525
E-Mail: napps@ahint.com
www.petsitters.org

Pet Sitters International
201 East King Street
King, NC 27021-9161
Telephone: (336) 983-9222
Fax: (336) 983-5266
E-Mail: info@petsit.com
www.petsit.com

RESCUE ORGANIZATIONS AND ANIMAL WELFARE GROUPS

American Humane Association (AHA)
63 Inverness Drive East
Englewood, CO 80112
Telephone: (303) 792-9900
Fax: 792-5333
www.americanhumane.org

American Society for the Prevention of Cruelty to Animals (ASPCA)
424 E. 92nd Street
New York, NY 10128-6804
Telephone: (212) 876-7700
www.aspca.org

The Humane Society of the United States (HSUS)
2100 L Street, NW
Washington DC 20037
Telephone: (202) 452-1100
www.hsus.org

Royal Society for the Prevention of Cruelty to Animals (RSPCA)
RSPCA Enquiries Service
Wilberforce Way, Southwater,
Horsham, West Sussex RH13 9RS
United Kingdom
Telephone: 0870 3335 999
Fax: 0870 7530 284
www.rspca.org.uk

SPORTS

International Agility Link (IAL)
Global Administrator: Steve Drinkwater
E-Mail: yunde@powerup.au
www.agilityclick.com/~ial

The World Canine Freestyle Organization, Inc.
P.O. Box 350122
Brooklyn, NY 11235
Telephone: (718) 332-8336
Fax: (718) 646-2686
E-Mail: WCFODOGS@aol.com
www.worldcaninefreestyle.org

THERAPY

Delta Society
875 124th Ave, NE, Suite 101
Bellevue, WA 98005
Telephone: (425) 679-5500
Fax: (425) 679-5539
E-Mail: info@DeltaSociety.org
www.deltasociety.org

Therapy Dogs Inc.
P.O. Box 20227
Cheyenne WY 82003
Telephone: (877) 843-7364
Fax: (307) 638-2079
E-Mail: therapydogsinc@
qwestoffice.net
www.therapydogs.com

Therapy Dogs International (TDI)
88 Bartley Road
Flanders, NJ 07836
Telephone: (973) 252-9800
Fax: (973) 252-7171
E-Mail: tdi@gti.net
www.tdi-dog.org

TRAINING

Association of Pet Dog Trainers (APDT)
101 North Main Street, Suite 610
Greenville, SC 29601
Telephone: 1-(800) PET-DOGS
Fax: (864) 331-0767
E-Mail: information@apdt.com
www.apdt.com

International Association of Animal Behavior Consultants (IAABC)
565 Callery Road
Cranberry Township, PA 16066
E-Mail: info@iaabc.org
www.iaabc.org

National Association of Dog Obedience Instructors (NADOI)
PMB 369
729 Grapevine Hwy.
Hurst, TX 76054-2085
www.nadoi.org

VETERINARY AND HEALTH RESOURCES

Academy of Veterinary Homeopathy (AVH)
P.O. Box 9280
Wilmington, DE 19809
Telephone: (866) 652-1590
Fax: (866) 652-1590
www.theavh.org

American Academy of Veterinary Acupuncture (AAVA)
P.O. Box 1058
Glastonbury, CT 06033
Telephone: (860) 632-9911
Fax: (860) 659-8772
www.aava.org

American Animal Hospital Association (AAHA)
12575 W. Bayaud Ave.
Lakewood, CO 80228
Telephone: (303) 986-2800
Fax: (303) 986-1700
E-Mail: info@aahanet.org
www.aahanet.org/index.cfm

American College of Veterinary Internal Medicine (ACVIM)
1997 Wadsworth Blvd., Suite A
Lakewood, CO 80214-5293
Telephone: (800) 245-9081
Fax: (303) 231-0880
Email: ACVIM@ACVIM.org
www.acvim.org

American College of Veterinary Ophthalmologists (ACVO)
P.O. Box 1311
Meridian, ID 83860
Telephone: (208) 466-7624
Fax: (208) 466-7693
E-Mail: office09@acvo.com
www.acvo.com

American Holistic Veterinary Medical Association (AHVMA)
2218 Old Emmorton Road
Bel Air, MD 21015
Telephone: (410) 569-0795
Fax: (410) 569-2346
E-Mail: office@ahvma.org
www.ahvma.org

American Veterinary Medical Association (AVMA)
1931 North Meacham Road, Suite 100
Schaumburg, IL 60173-4360
Telephone: (847) 925-8070
Fax: (847) 925-1329
E-Mail: avmainfo@avma.org
www.avma.org

ASPCA Animal Poison Control Center
Telephone: (888) 426-4435
www.aspca.org

British Veterinary Association (BVA)
7 Mansfield Street
London
W1G 9NQ
Telephone: 0207 636 6541
Fax: 0207 908 6349
E-Mail: bvahq@bva.co.uk
www.bva.co.uk

Canine Eye Registration Foundation (CERF)
VMDB/CERF
1717 Philo Rd
P O Box 3007
Urbana, IL 61803-3007
Telephone: (217) 693-4800
Fax: (217) 693-4801
E-Mail: CERF@vmbd.org
www.vmdb.org

Orthopedic Foundation for Animals (OFA)
2300 NE Nifong Blvd
Columbus, Missouri 65201-3856
Telephone: (573) 442-0418
Fax: (573) 875-5073
Email: ofa@offa.org
www.offa.org

US Food and Drug Administration Center for Veterinary Medicine (CVM)
7519 Standish Place
HFV-12
Rockville, MD 20855-0001
Telephone: (240) 276-9300 or (888) INFO-FDA
http://www.fda.gov/cvm

PUBLICATIONS
BOOKS

Anderson, Teoti. *The Super Simple Guide to Housetraining*. Neptune City: TFH Publications, 2004.

Anne, Jonna, with Mary Straus. *The Healthy Dog Cookbook: 50 Nutritious and Delicious Recipes Your Dog Will Love*. UK: Ivy Press Limited, 2008.

Dainty, Suellen. *50 Games to Play With Your Dog*. UK: Ivy Press Limited, 2007.

Ewing, Susan M. *Animal Planet Cavalier King Charles Spaniels.* Neptune City: TFH Publications, Inc., 2007.

Savant-Harris, Myra. *Terra-Nova The Cavalier King Charles Spaniel.* Neptune City: TFH Publications, Inc., 2010.

Spiotta-DiMare, Loren. *DogLife Cavalier King Charles Spaniel.* Neptune City: TFH Publications, Inc., 2011.

MAGAZINES

AKC Family Dog
American Kennel Club
260 Madison Avenue
New York, NY 10016
Telephone: (800) 490-5675
E-Mail: familydog@akc.org
www.akc.org/pubs/familydog

AKC Gazette
American Kennel Club
260 Madison Avenue
New York, NY 10016
Telephone: (800) 533-7323
E-Mail: gazette@akc.org
www.akc.org/pubs/gazette

Dog & Kennel
Pet Publishing, Inc.
7-L Dundas Circle
Greensboro, NC 27407
Telephone: (336) 292-4272
Fax: (336) 292-4272
E-Mail: info@petpublishing.com
www.dogandkennel.com

Dogs Monthly
Ascot House
High Street, Ascot,
Berkshire SL5 7JG
United Kingdom
Telephone: 0870 730 8433
Fax: 0870 730 8431
E-Mail: admin@rtc-associates.freeserve.co.uk
www.corsini.co.uk/dogsmonthly

WEBSITES

Nylabone
www.nylabone.com

TFH Publications, Inc.
www.tfh.com

BIBLIOGRAPHY

CHAPTER 1: ORIGINS
Clubs
AKC
www.akc.org

ACKCSC USA
www.ackcsc.org

CKCSC USA
www.ckcsc.org

CKCSC Canada
www.cavaliercanada.com

CKCSC Great Britain
www.thecavalierclub.co.uk/start.html

Rescue
ACKCSC USA Rescue
www.ackcsc.org/about/rescue.html

CKCSC USA Rescue
www.ckcsc.org/ckcsc/ckcsc_inc.nsf/Founded-1954/rescue.html

CHAPTER 2: CHARACTERISTICS
See club sites in Chapter 1 above for breed standard and other information.

CHAPTER 4: FEEDING
Bones and Raw Food
Billinghurst, *Dr. Ian. Give Your Dog a Bone: The Practical Commonsense Way to Feed Dogs for a Long Healthy Life.* Ian Billinghurst, 1993.

Billinghurst, Dr. Ian. *Grow Your Pups with Bones: The BARF Program For breeding Healthy Dogs And Eliminating Skeletal Disease.* Ian Billinghurst, 1998.

Lonsdale, Tom. *Raw Meaty Bones Promote Health.* Dogwise Publishing, 2001.

Home-Cooked
Pitcairn, Richard H., DVM, PhD, and Susan Hubble Pitcairn. *Complete Guide to Natural Health for Dogs and Cats.* New York: Rodale Books, 2005.

Segal, Monica. *Optimal Nutrition Raw and Cooked Canine Diets: The Next Level.* Monica Segal, 2007.

Strombeck, Donald R, DVM, PhD. *Home-Prepared Dog & Cat Diets: The Healthful Alternative.* Hoboken: Wiley-Blackwell. Neptune City, 1999.

Websites
http://k9rawdiet.com/Optimal-Nutrition-Raw-and-Cooked-Canine-Diets-by-Monica-Segal-pr-250.html www.barfworld.com

CHAPTER 5: GROOMING
See Chapter 3 for sources of grooming supplies.

http://dryingcoat.com

http://groomingcoat.com

www.bathcoats.com/PageDogAp2.asp

CHAPTER 6: HEALTH
General
Cavalier InfoCenter Site
www.roycroftinformationcenter.com

2006 Vaccine Protocols
www.aahanet.org/PublicDocuments/VaccineGuidelines06Revised.pdf

Alternative Veterinary Care
www.ahvma.org

Canine Health Information Center (CHIC)
www.caninehealthinfo.org

Early Neuter/Spay Considerations
www.caninesports.com/SpayNeuter.html

Natural Rearing
www.naturalrearing.com/coda/index.html

The Orthopedic Foundation for Animals (OFA)
www.offa.org

Syringomyelia
http://sm.cavaliertalk.com

Pet Insurance
http://www.24petwatch.com/petinsurance

www.gopetplan.com

www.petinsurance.com/affiliates/PPCOVERTURE.aspx?ec=CI0134&src=ysm
www.petsbest.com

CHAPTER 7: TRAINING
Bite Inhibition link
http://deesdogs.com/documents/teachingbiteinhibition.pdf

www.crickethollowfarm.com/biteinhib.htm

www.whole-dog-journal.com/issues/13_6/features/Bite-Inhibition_16232-1.html

Canine Discipline link
http://roycroftinformationcenter.com/manualcaninedisciplinearticle.htm

Clicker Training
www.clickertraining.com
www.youtube.com/watch?v=IC367wKGi4M

CHAPTER 8: PROBLEM BEHAVIORS
Bach's Rescue Remedy
www.rescueremedy.com

Lost Dog
www.petamberalert.com

Sound Desensitization links
http://calmaudio.com
www.gentleleader.ca/densensitization.html

CHAPTER 9: SPORTS AND ACTIVITIES
Canine Good Citizen (CGC)
www.akc.org/events/cgc/training-testing.cfm

Flyball
http://flyball.org

Lure Coursing
http://www.akc.org/events/lure_coursing

Performance
www.akc.org/pdfs/events/GOCET1.pdf

Showing
AKC: www.akc.org/events/conformation/beginners.cfm
CKCSC: www.ckcsc.org/ckcsc/ckcsc_inc.nsf/Founded-1954/showing.html

Therapy Work
Delta Society
www.deltasociety.org

Therapy Dogs International (TDI)
www.tdi-dog.org

Pet-Friendly Hotel links
www.pet-friendly-hotels.net
www.petswelcome.com
www.officialpethotels.com

Magazines
The Royal Spaniels
http://the-royal-spaniels.com

The Whole Dog Journal
www.whole-dog-journal.com

INDEX

Note: Boldfaced numbers indicate an illustration.

A

accidents, housetraining, 100–102
activities. *See also* sports
    Canine Good Citizen program, 123–124
    therapy work, 126–127, **127**
    traveling with your Cavalier, 126, 128–130, **128**, **131**
acupuncture, 87
adaptability, 21
adoption of puppies, 17
affectionateness, 21, **24**
age expectancy, 88
agility events, 122–123, **122**
air travel, 129
Alansmere Aquarius (Cavalier), 12
allergies, 49–50, 86, **86**
alternative therapies, 87–88
Alzheimer's disease, 89
Amanda Loo of Ttiweh, Ch. (Cavalier), 10
American Association of Feed Control Officials (AAFCO), 41
American Cavalier King Charles Spaniel Club (ACKCSC), 13
American Kennel Club (AKC)
    agility levels, 123
    Cavalier recognition in, 11–13
    conformation points, 124
    obedience titles, 125–126
    rally levels, 126
anesthesia, 66, 67
Ann's Son (Cavalier), 9, 10
annual veterinarian visits, 71

B

Bach's Rescue Remedy, 118, 119
balanced diet, 39–41, **40**, **44**
BARF (bones and raw food) diet, 45
barking, 110–112
bathing, 58–60, **59–60**
bedding, 28–29, **28**
behavior problems

barking, 110–112
chewing, 112–113, **112**
digging, 113–114, **113**
house soiling, 114–115
jumping up, 115–116
lead pulling, 116–117, **117**
mouthing/nipping, 116
separation anxiety, 117–118
sound sensitivity, 118–119
behaviorists, 119, **119**
Bertie of Rookerynook (Cavalier), 10
Biologically Appropriate Raw Food (BARF), 45
biting, play, 116
black and tan Cavaliers, **19**, 20, **20**
Blenheim color, 18–20, **19**
Blenheim spot, 8, 19, 20
blindness, 89
boarding your Cavalier, 130–131
body language, 93
body structure, 17
bones, care of, 79, 83, 89
bones and raw food (BARF) diet, 45
bordetella (kennel cough), 74
bowls, food and water, 32–33, **32**
breed club rescue organizations, 17
breeders/breeding, 24
breed-specific health issues, 78–86
bristle brushes, **54**, 55
Brown, Gertrude (Trudy) Polk, 11
Brown, Sally Lyons, 11
brushing
    coat, 57–58, **58**
    teeth, 65–66

C

cancer, 67, 72, 86
canine cognitive dysfunction (CCD), 89
Canine Good Citizen (CGC) program, 123–124
canned foods, 43, **43**
car seat/harness/crate, 29
car travel, 128–129
carbohydrates in diet, 39
Cavalier King Charles Spaniel Club (CKCSC), 9, 124

Cavalier King Charles Spaniel Club, USA (CKCSC, USA), 10–11, 12–13, 124
chain leashes, 34
characteristics of Cavaliers. *See also* living with your Cavaliers
    body structure, 17
    coat, 17–18
    colors, 18–21, **19–20**
    general traits, 16–17, **16**, 23–24
    head, **16**
    size, 17
    temperament, **7**, 21–23
checkups, health, 71, 88
chewing, 112–113, **112**
children and Cavaliers, 22, **22**
chiropractic treatment, 88
clicker training, 92
coat
    care of, 57–62, **58–60**
    characteristics of, 17–18
    colors of, 18–21, **19–20**
collars, 29, 92, **92**
colors of Cavaliers
    black and tan, **19**, 20, **20**
    blenheim, 18–20, **19**
    ruby, **19**, 20–21
    tricolor, 18, **19**, 20
Come (recall) command, 103–104, **103**
commands. *See also* training
    Come (recall), 103–104, **103**
    Down, 104–105, **105**
    Heel, 106–107
    Off, 116
    Quiet, 112
    Sit command, 102–103
    Speak, 111
    Stay, 105–106
commercial diets, 38–39, 41–44, **42**, **43**
commercial raw food diet, 44
companionability, 22–23, **22**, **24**
conformation (showing) events, 124, **124**
convulsions, 81
core vaccines, 73–74, **73**

coronavirus, 74
crate dish (for water), 33
crate training, 95–97, **96**
crates, 29–31, **30**

D
Daywell Nell (Cavalier), 9
Daywell Roger, Ch. (Cavalier), 9
Delta Society, 126
dental care, 65–66, **65**, 89
diet. *See* feeding
digestive system, 38–39
digging, 32, 113–114, **113**
diseases. *See* health issues
distemper, 73
Down command, 104–105, **105**
dry dog food (kibble), 41–42, **42**
drying coat, 61
dysplasia, hip, 79

E
ears
    care of, 55, 59, 63–64, **63**
    problems with, 87, **87**, 89
Eldridge, Roswell, 9
emergency care, 81
end-of-life issues, 89
environment, living, 23
epilepsy, 78
episodic falling syndrome (EFS),
    78, **79**
exercise pens (x-pens), 35
exercise requirements, 23, **50**, 51
eye care, 64

F
fats in diet, 39–40, **40**
feeding
    additions to diet, 45–47, **46**
    allergies to food, 49–50
    balanced diet, 39–41, **40**, **44**
    commercial diets, 38–39, 41–44,
        42, **43**
    digestive system, 38–39
    noncommercial diets, 44–45
    obesity and, **49**, 50–51, **50**, 60
    puppies and, 31
    quantity of, **38**, **47**, 48–49, 51

schedule for, 45, 47–48
senior dogs and, 88–89
vitamin/mineral supplements,
    45, 46, 79
vitamins/minerals in diet,
    40–41
female dogs, 23–24, 48
fencing, 31–32
flea combs, 55
fleas, 76–77, **76**
fly catcher's syndrome, 78
flyball events, 125
food bowls, 32–33, **32**
Foster, Katherine, 12

G
gates, 33
gender, 23–24, 48
groomers, professional, 62, 67, **67**
grooming
    coat care, 57–62, **58–60**
    dental care, 65–66, **65**, 89
    ear care, 55, 59, 63–64, **63**
    eye care, 64
    importance of, 54
    nail care, **61**, 62–63
    for senior dogs, 66–67, **66**
    supplies, 33, 54–57, **54**, **56–57**
grooming table, 57, **57**

H
harnesses, 29
head, characteristics of, **16**
health issues. *See also* alternative
    therapies
    allergies, 49–50, 86, **86**
    breeders and, 24
    cancer, 67, 72, 86
    canine cognitive dysfunction,
        89
    convulsions, 81
    ear problems, 87, **87**, 89
    epilepsy, 78
    episodic falling syndrome, 78,
        79
    fly catcher's syndrome, 78
    heatstroke, 81
    hip dysplasia, 79

hypoglycemia, 81
hypothermia, 81
keratoconjunctivitis sicca,
    79–80
mitral valve disease, 65, 70,
    80–83, **82**
neutering, 24, 55, 60, 72
parasites, 76–78
patellar luxation, 83
primary secretory otitis media,
    83
reverse sneezing, 84
seizures, 81
senior dogs, 88–89, **88**
shock, 81
spaying, 24, 55, 60, 72
syringomyelia, 84–85, **84**, 86
thrombocytopenia, 85
umbilical hernias, 85–86
vaccinations. *see* vaccinations
wounds, open, 81
hearing loss, 89
heart problems, 65, 70, 80–83, **82**
heartworms, 77
heatstroke, 81
Heel command, 106–107
hepatitis, 73
herbal remedies, 88
hip dysplasia, 79
home-cooked diets, 45
homopathy, 88, 118, 119
hookworms, 77
House of Stuart and Cavaliers, 6–7
house soiling, 114–115
housetraining, 98–102, **98–99**, **101**
hypoglycemia, 81
hypothermia, 81

I
identification (ID) items, 33–34
illnesses. *See* health issues
incontinence, 89
It Takes a Thief (television show),
    23

J
joints, care of, 79, 83, 89
Jumpers and Weavers classes, 123

jumping up, 115–116

K
Kennel Club (KC), 9, 124
kennel cough (bordetella), 74
keratoconjunctivitis sicca (KCS), 79–80
kibble (dry dog food), 41–42, **42**
Kilspindie Lawmaker, UD (Cavalier), 12
King Charles II and Cavaliers, 6–7

L
laparoscopic spaying procedure, 72
Lawmaker (Cavalier), 100–102
lead pulling behavior, 116–117, **117**
leashes, 34, **34**, 92
leptospirosis, 75
living with your Cavaliers. *See also* characteristics of Cavaliers
  adaptability, 21
  affectionateness, 21, **24**
  companionability, 22–23, **22**, **24**
  environment, 23
  exercise requirements, 23, **50**, 51
  gender, 23–24, 48
  health, 24. *see also* health issues
  protectiveness, 23, 25
  temperament, **7**, 21–23
  trainability, 25, 92, **94**
lodgings, pet friendly, 129–139, **130**
lure coursing events, 125
Lyme disease, 75, **75**

M
male dogs, 23–24, 48
marker words, 92
Marlborough Spaniel, 8
Master Agility Championship (MACH) title, 123
medical emergencies, 81
Mercury of Eyeworth (Cavalier), 11
microchip identification, 33–34
minerals in diet, 40–41, 45, 46, 79
Miss Eda of Manscross, CD (Cavalier), 12
mitral valve disease (MVD), 65, 70,
80–83, **82**
mouthing/nipping, 116

N
nail care, **61**, 62–63
nail clippers, 56–57, **56**
neutering, 24, 55, 60, 72
nipping, 116
noise phobia, 118–119
noncommercial diets, 44–45
noncore vaccines, 74–75
nutritional needs, 39–41, **40**, **44**. *See also* feeding

O
obedience classes, 94, 107
obedience training, 102–107, **102**, **106**
obedience trials, 125–126, **125**
obesity, **49**, 50–51, **50**, 60
Off command, 116
origins of your Cavalier
  current status, 13
  early development, 6–8
  resurrection of breed, 9–10
  in United States, **9**, 10–13, **10**
other pets and Cavaliers, 22–23, 31

P
parainfluenza, 75
parasites, 76–78
Pargeter Lotus of Kilspindie (Cavalier), 11
Pargeter Mermaid (Cavalier), 11
parti-color Cavaliers, 18, 20
Partridge Wood Laughing Misdemeanor, Ch. (Cavalier), 13
parvovirus, 74
patellar luxation, 83
performance sports. *See* sports
pet sitters, 130–131
pin brushes, 55
popularity of Cavaliers, 12–13, **12**
positive training methods, 93, **94**
primary secretory otitis media (PSOM), 83
professionals. *See also* veterinarians

behaviorists, 119, **119**
groomers, 62, 67, **67**
trainers, 107
protectiveness, 23, 25
protein in diet, 40
Psyche of Eyeworth (Cavalier), 11
puppies
  adoption of, 17
  crates and, 114
  eating and, 41
  eye tearing and, 64
  feeding and, 31
  health problems and, 77
  other pets and, 31
  performance events and, 123
  table training, 95
  training sessions, 104, 111
puppy mills, 17

Q
quantity of food, **38**, **47**, 48–49, 51
Queen Victoria and Cavaliers, 8, **8**
Quiet command, 112

R
rabies, 74
rally events, 126
raw food diets, 44, 45
Recall (come) command, 103–104, **103**
rescue puppies, 17
retractable leashes, 34
reverse sneezing, 84
rib test (obesity), 50–51
Robrull of Veren, (Cavalier), 10
roundworms, 77
ruby color, **19**, 20–21

S
schedules
  feeding, 45, 47–48
  vaccinations, 75–76
Schiff, Mrs. John, 10
scissors, 56
scraps, feeding, 47
seizures, 81
semi-moist dog foods, 43–44
senility, 89

senior dogs
    grooming for, 66–67, **66**
    health issues, 88–89, **88**
separation anxiety, 117–118
Shaggymeads Lord Chancellor, UD
    (Cavalier), 12
shampoos, 58–59
shedding, 18, 57, 58
shock, 81
showing (conformation) events,
    124, **124**
sight loss, 89
Sit command, 102–103
size
    of Cavaliers, 17
    of crates, 31, 96–97
slicker brushes, 55
SM (syringomyelia), 84–85, **84**, 86
sneezing, reverse, 84
socialization, 95
sound sensitivity, 118–119
Spalding, Elizabeth, 11, 12
spaniel bowls (food and water), 33
spaying, 24, 55, 60, 72
Speak command, 111
sports activities. See also activities
    agility, 122–123, **122**
    conformation (showing), 124,
        124
    flyball, 125
    lure coursing, 125
    obedience trials, 125–126, **125**
    rally events, 126
    tracking, 127
Stay command, 105–106
stripping knife/comb, 55, 60
supplements
    for bones/joints, 79, 83, 89
    to diet, 45–47, **46**
    vitamin/mineral, 45, 46, 79
supplies
    bedding, 28–29, **28**
    bowls, food and water, 32–33,
        32
    brushes, **54**, 55
    car seat/harness/crate, 29
    collars, 29, 92, **92**

combs, 54–55, 60
crates, 29–31, **30**
dog food, 31. see also feeding
drying coat, 61
fencing, 31–32
gates, 33
    for grooming, 33, 54–57, **54**,
        56–57
identification (ID) items, 33–34
leashes, 34, **34**, 92
nail clippers, 56–57, **56**
scissors, 56
toothbrushes/toothpaste, 65
toys, 35, **35**
for training, 92–93
X-pens, 35
syringomyelia (SM), 84–85, **84**, 86

T
temperament, **7**, 21–23
Therapy Dogs International (TDI),
    126
therapy work, 126–127, **127**
thrombocytopenia, 85
ticks, 76–77, **76**
toothbrushes/toothpaste, 65. See
    also dental care
toys, 35, **35**
tracking events, 127
trainability, 25, 92, **94**
trainers, professional, 107
training. See also commands
    crate training, 95–97, **96**
    housetraining, 98–102, **98–99**,
        101
    importance of, 92
    obedience, basic, 102–107, **102**,
        106
    obedience classes, 94, 107
    socialization, 95
    tips for, 92–94
traveling with your Cavalier, 126,
    128–130, **128**, **131**
treats, 47, 92–93
tricolor Cavaliers, 18, **19**, 20

U
umbilical hernias, 85–86

United States, breed origins in, **9**,
    10–13, **10**

V
vacations. See traveling with your
    Cavalier
vaccinations. See also health issues
    bordetella, 74
    coronavirus, 74
    distemper, 73
    hepatitis, 73
    leptospirosis, 75
    Lyme disease, 75, **75**
    parainfluenza, 75
    parvovirus, 74
    rabies, 74
    schedule for, 75–76
vegetables in diet, 46, **46**
vehicle traffic and Cavaliers, 18
vehicles, traveling in, 29, 128–129
veterinarians
    health checkups, 71, 88
    locating, 70
    teeth cleaning and, 66
vision loss, 89
vitamins in diet, 40–41, 45, 46, 79

W
waist test (obesity), 51
walk nicely on leash (heel
    command), 106–107
water bowls, 32–33, **32**
water requirements, 41
whipworms, 77–78
Whitman, Mrs. Harold, 10
whole food diets, 38–39
whole-color Cavaliers, 18
William of Orange and Mary and
    Cavaliers, 7–8
worms, 77–78
wounds, open, 81

X
X-pen, 35

PHOTO CREDITS

DEDICATION

To my many Cavaliers who helped me learn so much over the years and in turn helped me do a better job raising my human children.

ACKNOWLEDGMENTS

Thanks to the Cavalier breed clubs that continue to try to protect the welfare of this lovely breed.

ABOUT THE AUTHOR

Laura Lang has been showing and breeding Cavaliers for 35 years. She has been an active member of the Cavalier King Charles Spaniel Club-USA (CKCSC, USA) since 1976 and has served in offices in both the national and Midwest regional clubs, was Show Secretary many times, and was a past Show Chairperson. She also designs and maintains many websites, including one for Cavaliers of the Northeast. Laura has lived in the Cleveland, Ohio, area all her life. She has two grown children and still shares her home with eight Cavaliers. Her breeding philosophy reflects her interest in health and genetics and especially the love she has for the breed.

ABOUT ANIMAL PLANET™

Animal Planet™ is the only television network dedicated exclusively to the connection between humans and animals. The network brings people of all ages together by tapping into our fundamental fascination with animals through an array of fresh programming that includes humor, competition, drama, and spectacle from the animal kingdom.

ABOUT *DOGS 101*

The most comprehensive—and most endearing—dog encyclopedia on television, *DOGS 101* spotlights the adorable, the feisty and the unexpected. A wide-ranging rundown of everyone's favorite dog breeds—from the Dalmatian to Xoloitzcuintli —this series surveys a variety of breeds for their behavioral quirks, genetic history, most famous examples and wildest trivia. Learn which dogs are best for urban living and which would be the best fit for your family. Using a mix of animal experts, pop-culture footage and stylized dog photography, *DOGS 101* is an unprecedented look at man's best friend.